A Bible Convention in Congo

CONGO SAGA

First published   SEPTEMBER 1965
Reprinted   JANUARY 1966

CONGO SAGA

*An authentic record of
the Heroes of the Cross
during the 'Simba' rising*

DAVID W. TRUBY

UNEVANGELIZED FIELDS MISSION
9 GUNNERSBURY AVENUE, LONDON, W.5.

Dedicated to those
who laid down their lives
during the 'Simba' rising, 1964

MARTYRS

(Dedicated to the Martyrs of the 20th Century)

Dare we forget the martyrs' heavy toll,
  When, by their blood, Christ's banner they unroll?
Rome's sands, for pleasure soaked in sacred red,
  That o'er the world the Light of Christ be shed.

Has His dear church no tears that she can shed,
  That she so little values gems of the martyred dead?
His Word — the Lamp and Guide of many weary feet,
  To-day despised, as if t'was written to deceive and cheat.

The cry of saints now long ago laid low,
  Their blood it speaks — the earth but echoes back their groans,
"Why was the Coliseum's sands our grave?" the martyr cries,
  "Why have you sold the cause that cost our lives?"

The Cause of Truth calls forth yet once again
  The lives of the sweetest — death to them must be undying
    gain.
The fight is on, but time is sinking fast,
  Martyrs again — but they may be the last!

Oh! for the joy when worlds, now wrecked with sin,
  No more shall shed the life blood of our kith and kin,
When God and saints, one family complete, shall know the
    names
  Of those who laid their lives at His dear feet.

Leonard F. Harris.
June, 1940.

3

Printed by Wright's (Sandbach) Ltd., Cheshire

CONTENTS

FOREWORD

IT IS A VERY real privilege to write a Foreword to this book. The whole story of the sufferings of men and women in Congo, and particularly in the North East Province, during the upheavals of 1964/65 will probably never be told, but in this book Mr. Truby has gathered together much valuable material, and given us an overall picture of the situation. Some of us who have been in close touch with missionaries who escaped from Congo at that time will never be able to forget the impression they made upon us. Here were men and women who "counted not their lives dear unto them". Many of them were anxious to return at the earliest possible opportunity to the field of their labours. A number of Missions suffered grievous casualties in this tragic blood-bath, but no Mission sustained heavier casualties than the Unevangelized Fields Mission. The Mission lost some of her choicest personnel. Men and women, young and old, single ladies and missionary families suffered alike. Yet, when all this has been recorded there must inevitably be many gaps in the story. Missionaries are loath to tell of their experiences, and tend to make light of their sufferings. The words at the conclusion of the eleventh chapter of the Epistle to the Hebrews seem strangely appropriate — "Others were tortured not accepting deliverance; that they might obtain a better resurrection: and others had trial of cruel mockings and scourgings, yea, moreover of bonds and imprisonment: they were stoned, they were sawn asunder, were tempted, were slain with the sword: they wandered about in sheepskins and goatskins; being destitute, afflicted, tormented." Such words were literally true in the experience of many of these remarkable men and women. It might seem incredible to some that, in the middle of the twentieth century, such sufferings should have been inflicted by men and women on their fellow creatures, but that which is recorded here can

6

be substantiated, and there is a great deal more that cannot be recorded which only serves to underline the depths to which fallen human nature can sink, apart from the grace of God. As Mr. Truby has pointed out, however, this is only one side of the story for there were remarkable acts of heroism on the part of Congolese Christians in which they risked their own lives for the sake of their missionary friends. The Congolese Church suffered proportionately far greater than did the missionary force, yet Christians remain faithful to their Lord.

Once again the saying has been proved true — that the blood of the martyrs is the seed of the Church. We have been reminded that it is still a costly business to follow the Lord Jesus Christ, but we recall the promise of His Word that "If we suffer with Him we shall also reign with Him". It is not without significance that the Greek word which is translated "witness" in the New Testament is also literally transcribed into the English language in the word "martyr". We have been forcibly reminded that there are times when the cost of witnessing is in fact martyrdom.

GILBERT W. KIRBY.

30 *Bedford Place,*
*London, W.C.*1.

JUNE, 1965.

"Saga" is the Icelandic word meaning "to say", and was originally used in connection with manuscripts written between the years 1,000 A.D. and 1,300 A.D. dealing with the deeds of heroes of Iceland, mainly recording their adventures at sea and their voyages towards America. These sagas, both historical and mythical, give a good picture of life in the island as it was at the time.

CONGO SAGA

CHAPTER ONE

THE LAIR OF THE LIONS

A SERIES OF victorious cries from the direction of the Aruwimi
River awoke the town of Banalia to sudden action. "Crocodile,
crocodile" came the cries; and still louder cries summoning
the men to race to the river bank to witness the death of an
enemy. Amid the confusion of shouts, orders, and running
hither and thither, a young missionary from Glasgow, William
Gilvear, joined the race to the river bank, and he was just in
time to see the kill. Chanting and shouting they pulled a
huge crocodile entangled in a trap, on to the land. But the
crocodile still had plenty of life in it. As it reached dry land
it ran and snapped at the nearest man only to be dragged in
the opposite direction before it could close its jaws. Spears
were thrown trying to find a vulnerable point in the brute's
scaly armour. "Crocodile, crocodile" again pierced the air
together with other calls, "kill, kill". Twisting, turning,
snapping with its entangled jaws and beating with its huge
tail, the crocodile made a fight for life. William Gilvear
stood rooted to the spot next to an elderly Congolese who,
owing to his advanced years, was unable to take part in the
sport. Suddenly a spear found the eye of the crocodile and
the creature opened its huge jaws revealing two long rows
of shimmering teeth as it snorted in agony. Immediately the
jaws were open a dozen other spears were plunged down its
throat and minutes later the crocodile lay still on the sands.

"He is dead, he is dead" re-echoed the river bank and
messengers ran off to the village of Banalia to convey the
news. Out came the knives and machettes, huge double-
bladed knives traditionally used by the Congolese on their
enemies and for many other purposes. Rapidly they hacked
through the thick armour of the crocodile and cut its flesh
into joints. Bill Gilvear watched in amazement.

"What are they going to do with it now?" he asked the
elderly man who stood near him still surveying the scene.

"We are going to eat him," replied the man, "already
the women are lighting the fires."

"What! You eat the flesh of a crocodile?" queried Bill
Gilvear.

The man's face broke into a toothless grin. "He is our
enemy," was the reply, "he ate our forefathers, he eats us,
now we eat him in anger."

"Does the crocodile make good meat?" asked the
astounded missionary.

"The crocodile tastes like big fish. It doesn't matter if it
is good nor not. He is our enemy. This is our way," said
the delighted Congolese with a ring of victory in his voice
as he turned to make his way to the village and to claim
a portion of the roasted meat.

For five years William Gilvear had been praying for Congo,
and this was his introduction to the country. He had heard
much about this immense land of over 900,000 square miles,
in which 15 million people lived. He had heard that Herodotus
had written about it five centuries before the birth of Christ
and had mentioned "the mountains of the moon", doubt-
lessly referring to the Ruwenzori Range and its "little people",
the pygmies. Although the Equator runs through the country
giving it an average temperature of 77 degrees F. yet the
Ruwenzori mountains are snow capped throughout the year.
This, then, was the land to which God had called him to
bear witness to the name of Jesus Christ, and these were the

people for whom he was burdened, and to whom he was to preach the unsearchable riches of Christ. As he drove slowly back to his station he thought of the traditional mentality of these people who would eat the flesh of their enemy in anger, and he realised, for the first time, what a gigantic task was ahead of him; nor could he help wondering why hatred was entrenched so deeply. William Gilvear set himself the task of probing into the background of the people and discovered that the comparatively short history of Congo was by no means happy and the Congolese had received brutal treatment by many.

Up to the latter part of the eighteenth century the interior of Africa was largely unknown and unexplored. The Congo Basin remained the *"Terra-ignota"*. Livingstone and Stanley penetrated into the heart of this dark continent between the years 1874 and 1877 and in the subsequent scramble for Africa, King Leopold of Belgium took over Congo as his private estate. In 1885 it became the Congo Free State, and Belgium began to administer it as a colony in 1908, but when Stanley arrived he found that other white men had preceded him. For almost fifty years Arab slave traders and merchants seeking both gold and ivory had penetrated far into Congo, pillaging, raiding and massacring all who tried to resist them in their quest for spoils of white ivory, pure gold and black life. Fear and tyranny reigned among the primitive peoples of Congo through the unscrupulous Arab chief, Hammed Ben-Mohammed, more commonly known as Tippo Tip. On one occasion Livingstone testified that he saw slave traders shoot into a crowd killing and wounding men, women and children. In 1888 the Belgian Anti-Slavery Society was founded by Cardinal Lavigerie specifically to suppress the slave trade in Central Africa. Bitter fighting broke out; there was a heavy loss of life among the Arab traders and the troops of the Free State and the Anti-Slave Society. It was not until September 22nd, 1894 that the last Arab bastion capitulated at Pweto (in the State now known as Katanga) and the Congolese were rid of the evil inflicted upon them.

Then followed seventy years of Belgian colonial rule. They
intended that both countries should develop to the mutual
advantage of each other. They ruled with a firm hand, built
cities, cultivated plantations, constructed roadways, railways,
bridges, and introduced all the benefits and advantages of
Western civilisation. They provided educational, medical
and social services and gradually the primitive darkness of
Congo began to disappear. But as the years passed by many
Congolese began to envy the superior position of their
colonisers and longed for the day when the country would
be independent and they would retain their own profits and be
free from the yoke of white rule. Many traders had been
indiscreet, unfair, and had taken advantage of the situation.
In the early years many had exploited the Congolese for
rubber, and atrocities had been committed. Very little reward
was given for hard labour and the molesting of Congolese
women was not unknown. In the late nineteen-fifties the
number of educated Congolese had increased rapidly and
pressure for independence became more pronounced. One
of the leaders, Patrice Lumumba, led a rebellion in an
endeavour to throw off Belgian domination, and demanded
that all whites withdraw under the threat of constant guerilla
warfare.

Belgium responded to the call for independence surprisingly
quickly and drew up a constitution and granted independence
on 30th June, 1960. In the first elections held, Lumumba
received an overwhelming majority and became the first
Prime Minister of the new nation. After only a few months
in power he was deposed and shortly afterwards cruelly
murdered. This sowed the seeds for further hostilities. Also,
shortly after independence, Moise Tshombe, who was in
power in Katanga, endeavoured to break away from the
Central Government and form an independently ruled province. The U.N. forces intervened and crushed the uprising,
banishing Tshombe. Three other Prime Ministers followed
each other in quick succession endeavouring to establish
peace, unity and prosperity, but were unsuccessful. All was

not well in Congo. Even though the Central Government had obtained a large majority in the elections a left-wing group had become rooted and was rapidly gaining power. Mr. Adoula, the third Prime Minister, in a genuine attempt to form a stable Government, called a Parliamentary conference at Lovanium in August 1961, but unhappily failed to satisfy the demands of this group, and thus a left-wing opposition party was formed which subsequently engaged in subversive activities and agitated against the Government, ignoring the constitution of the land and democratic principles of government. They caused unrest in all walks of life, organised local disturbances and even in Leopoldville there were criminal outrages and plastic bombs thrown. Following the usual procedure of Communist inspired activities, they infiltrated into the large centres of population and gradually gained power. Three successive revolts against the local authorities broke out in Kwilu, Lomami and Kivu.

The rebel group established their headquarters in Brazzaville, the capital city of the neighbouring Republic of Congo (formerly French Congo) and it was there in October 1963 that they created the organisation known as the National Liberation Committee (N.L.C.). The N.L.C. continued and increased its subversive activities until the country was in a state of disorganisation and unrest, and at this point Mr. Adoula resigned, and President Kasa-Vubu invited Dr. Moise Tshombe to form a "Government of Public Welfare" on 10th July, 1964, and instructed him to undertake the pacification of the country.

Thus, Mr. Tshombe took office at a critical time when the N.L.C. had already gained tremendous power. Mr. Tshombe decided on a "policy of broad reconciliation", and on July 19th, 1964, only nine days after accepting office, publicly stated: "My Government is, first of all, a Government of reconciliation. This is, of reconciliation on a national scale. Without this reconciliation peace will not be possible for the Congo. Each of you must not only understand this but work together so that we will no longer present abroad, and at home, a picture of a disunited family continually quarrelling". Tshombe then stated the immediate aims of his Government which were:—

1. to achieve national reconciliation and bring about general peace throughout the country;

2. to restore the economy and improve the financial position; and

3. to prepare for a General Election so that a Government of the choosing of the people could be constitutionally elected.

Tshombe then commenced a fervent attempt to carry out his policies and twice tried to visit Brazzaville but was prevented from doing so by the Government of the Republic of Congo — Brazzaville. By July 17th the Government of Public Welfare had liberated more than 2,000 political prisoners including Mr. Antoine Gizenga, the former Vice Prime Minister, who had been imprisoned for two and a half years. Then, Tshombe visited the eastern part of the country and continually asserted during this trip, "I have made appeals for peace and harmony. I still hope that they will be heard. I am against the use of force. I have said it, and I repeat it". However, the rebel leaders turned a deaf ear to the heart-cry of Tshombe and ignored his outstretched hand inviting reconciliation. In fact, they took advantage of this conciliatory spirit and openly attacked towns in the north and east of Congo. On August 5th they captured Stanleyville, thus geographically cutting off the north-eastern portion of the land. In spite of this open act of aggression, Prime Minister Tshombe declared on August 8th: "I am still leaving the door open for reconciliation but it must be understood that the patience of the Government has reached its limits. I have extended my hand for an entire month. Some responded to it, others profited by the situation to spread the rebellion. The Government cannot permit this".

*Fried Caterpillars—
a Congolese delicacy!*

*Women help in collecting leaves
for the roof of a new house.*

*This little child is kept well out of
mischief when she is put in her play-pen!*

*A party preparing to go hunting with
their nets, spears, and hunting dog.
Notice the bell around the dog's neck.*

*Graves of victims killed
during Arab slave raiding days.*

A pen and ink drawing by a Congolese national of a river scene.

The " Lumumba" monument, Stanleyville. Hundreds of Congolese were slain in front of the memorial to the deceased hero-leader.

The rebel leaders again ignored the invitation and a full scale rebellion broke out over the lovely land of Congo. Just as Israel refused God's call to repentance, "I have spread out my hands all the day unto a rebellious people, which walked in a way that was not good, after their own thoughts" (Isaiah 65, v. 2) so the rebels rejected the offer of the God-fearing Prime Minister — and the country headed towards disaster.

CHAPTER TWO

THE LIONS BEGIN TO ROAR

THE REBELLION was carefully planned and well organised. The basic training of the rebels took several months and was done in high secrecy. Several of the leaders went to Red China for specialist training, including Molele, who, on his return to Congo in 1963, organised the "Jeunesse" youth movement mainly by distributing literature. The rebels would send a group of young people into a village shouting and crying that the 'simbas' (the Swahili word for 'lions') were coming. A short time afterwards the lions would come with their bows and arrows, spears and guns, sow the seeds of fear, terrorise the population into accepting the movement and enlist as many men as possible to join their ranks. Because the population in many areas was dissatisfied with the government, they easily swung over to the rebel cause, particularly when guns were fired. The rebels then disposed of all local authorities, frequently burned administrative buildings and blocked the roads to prevent government soldiers reaching them. If a person openly opposed the rebels he was killed outright.

They had very rigid regulations among themselves and always greeted each other as "Camarade" (comrade). They roved the countryside in groups of 40-60 men and when two companies met they would advance with drawn bows and arrows toward each other while the scout asked where they had been, what they had done, where they were going, and what they were going to do when they got there. The scouts then returned to their leaders within the main company and then the two companies met or passed. Their discipline was strict. Each company had a "secretary" who kept an accurate record of the activities, including the misdemeanours of his men. These were reported to the "general" who sometimes ordered the offender to be punished. The usual punishment was to make the offender lie flat on his stomach while he was beaten mercilessly. The rebel leaders used both witchcraft and superstition to instil fear in their followers and in the areas which they succeeded in subduing. They told their Simba soldiers that if they were shot the bullets would turn to water when they were hit or if they did happen to die they would be resurrected after three days.

The medicine man also played his part. From the very commencement of the work of the U.F.M. in Congo, witchcraft was one of the greatest powers which the missionaries had to face. In 1903 when a small group of revolutionaries raised a standard against a Belgian administrator, they sent for a famous sorcerer who prepared a concoction from various herbs and the hearts of animals which was to be rubbed on their bodies which they believed would make them bullet proof. In the Simba rising, a similar story was spread. Provided they shouted 'Mai-ya-Mulele' (water of Mulele) the enemy bullets would not hurt them. When the Simbas marched on Stanleyville those leading the army of rebels were the medicine men, and when the Central Government troops saw the medicine men they fled for their lives. The Simbas had an ethical code of their own and, in fact, called themselves the Regime of Gentlemen. They had strict rules, such as no stealing, no adultery, no drunkenness, and they must face straight ahead when going into battle and must be careful not to step into the blood of the fallen. Their propaganda was second to none. "President" Gbenye continually broadcast to people within the territory he had subdued. Most of his speeches were simply diatribes against whites, particularly Belgians and Americans, and against any form of capitalism. On one occasion he said, "All men are born equal in that they come into the world with nothing. The forefathers of the white man dressed in leaves and skins but they progressed, and the time came when the Americans came to Africa to carry off the people as slaves. The Americans

were originally English who, seeing that America was a rich
country, left their homeland and went there. They killed off
all the redskins and took their land.

"After the slave raiders, came the Belgians, and though
they didn't carry away our people as slaves they reduced us
to slavery in another way. We had to work for very small
wages.

"Our great leader, Patrice Emery Lumumba, worked and
died for our liberation and won it, but some of our people
(the P.N.P. — *Partie National Populaire*) were simply animals.
When a man goes to hunt he takes his dog. It is also an
animal, and so catches the antelope or some other animal
for its owner. That is what the P.N.P. did. They acted as
the white man's dog which was fed by him so that he would
catch us and keep us under his power . . . "

As time progressed his propaganda grew more violent and
his policies more ruthless. He openly stated, "We will make
fetishes out of the hearts of Americans and Belgians and we
will dress ourselves in their skins". His colleague and
commander-in-chief of the rebel troops, "General" Nicolas
Olenga, said, "The Chinese communists have killed millions
and millions of people. This is why they succeeded. We must
follow their example". Moreover, their threats were far from
idle. At Stanleyville they assassinated the mayor, Mr. Leopold
Matabo, who was dismembered alive and eaten by rebel
cannibals; the provincial secretary, Mr. Gabriel Balete; the
former minister of the interior, Mr. Georges Kokonyange;
the director of the provincial ministry of interior, Mr. Pierre
Alamazani, and many others who had held high office or
who had been educated abroad or had associations with the
hated white capitalists, all met their deaths. In fact, more
than 2,000 Congolese were put to death in Stanleyville alone,
many before the huge Lumumba monument and nearly all
were the *elite* of the population. Similar outbreaks of violence
occurred throughout the rebel-held territory. In Kindu,
capital of the Maniema province, more than 800 office holders
were assassinated without any form of trial, while in Paulis

the governor, his provincial secretary, together with civil
servants, teachers, magistrates and office holders were executed
summarily. Some were forced to drink petrol after which
they were disemboweled and burned. More than 4,000
perished in the Paulis area and other killings occurred at
Bunia, Bumba, Uvira and Befale. Before one of the mass
executions, an eye witness testified that dance records were
played and youngsters of about ten years forced people
awaiting execution to eat the ballot papers of a recent con-
stitutional referendum. The rebels then set upon them with
sticks, machettes and guns. Their bodies were then loaded
on to wheelbarrows and thrown into the river not far away.

Despite the growing power of the rebels, most foreign
residents in Congo decided to remain, believing that as non-
combatants they would be permitted to carry on their normal
activities. Unfortunately this was not so. In spite of the
fact that the holding of hostages is contrary to all international
law, whites were prevented from leaving the territory and
later were placed under house arrest and later still many were
actually imprisoned in hotels, military camps and large
buildings. The significance of the hostages was two-fold.
Firstly, they were a bargaining point for peace. The rebel
leaders realised that their lives were in danger once they had
opened hostilities and hoped that they could use the presence
of a large number of white people as a lever with the Central
Government to agree to an amicable peace, whereby they
were given control over a large area of Congo. Secondly,
their purpose in holding white hostages was to prevent the
interference of Western countries in their "struggle for
liberty". While they stood a reasonable chance of success
of overthrowing the Central Government they knew only
too well they were no match for an organised and well-
equipped contingent of soldiers from Belgium, America,
Britain or United Nations. Thus, Gbenye stated quite openly
that if white soldiers were used against them the hostages
would be treated as prisoners of war and would be killed if
they were threatened by enforced capitulation.

CHAPTER THREE

THE FIRST U.F.M. DEATH IN CONGO

NORTH OF THE immense Ituri Forest there runs a road connecting the towns of Bumba, Ekoko and Aketi. One of the largest U.F.M. stations is at Ekoko and here there is a dispensary, a maternity hospital, a large primary school educating over four hundred children, a secondary school, a Bible school and a teachers' training college. There are often over fifteen missionaries engaged on this one station. The Sunday school at Ekoko has grown at a phenomenal rate and is not only attended by over 140 children but has also seen many conversions over the years. In addition to the central Sunday school another one is held outside the town to care for the children of the leprosy patients. More than 80 attend this week by week. The youth movements, "Lumieres" and "Flambeaux", are also strong on this station. Aketi has yielded a rich harvest of souls and there is a strong church there pastored by a national, and in nearly all the surrounding villages there are groups of believers. More than 60 national evangelists labour ceaselessly among them. Out of a total population of 14,000 more than 1,000 are active Christians and a prayer meeting is held every day at 6 a.m. which is attended by over 100 people. When the crisis cut off this area Joan Pengilly and Jean Raddon had already left for furlough and Jean Sweet had moved to the Boyulu station to spend the school vacation with her inseparable friend, Miss Olive McCarten. Thus at Ekoko there were: the Rev. and Mrs. William Scholten from Florida, U.S.A., with their five children, William "Ike" aged 8, Robbin aged 7, Stephen aged $4\frac{1}{2}$, Bruce aged 3, and Sandy aged $1\frac{1}{2}$ years; Miss Betty O'Neill from Ireland and Miss Pearl Hiles from the U.S.A. Also at Aketi there were Mr. and Mrs. Charles Mann, from the U.S.A. with their two children, Stephen aged 2½ and Cynthia aged 9 months. Only a few months before the crisis broke, all the stations had been equipped with a radio transmitter and these proved a tremendous asset until they were confiscated by the rebels.

Once the barriers had closed the missionaries continued to work as much as possible. Betty O'Neill repaired her sewing machine by pouring kettles of boiling water over it to remove the solidified oil and dust. Bill Scholten cleared the grounds of the Mission compound, whilst all helped in keeping the maternity work going. Regular Sunday services were held at the church and the Bible study group met during the week. On Wednesday, August 5th, Al Larson came through on the inter-station radio network loud and clear and told everyone of the deteriorating situation in Stanleyville. They decided to broadcast every two hours instead of every four and found that already Wanie Rukula had gone off the air. Old Michael, the Ekoko station evangelist, seemed very upset and sensed that something was wrong. By Saturday, August 8th, Ekoko station could still hear Al broadcasting though they themselves were unable to transmit. There was still no news from Wanie Rukula. On the 11th, Miss O'Neill heard from Dr. Sharpe at Bongondza over the radio who said that he had heard on the Stanleyville news that the rebels had called all radios in, and two days later Miss Olive Mc-Carten from Boyulu station reported that the situation was very tense indeed and they were expecting their transmitter to be confiscated at any minute. That same night Betty O'Neill was awakened in the early hours of the morning by Penny, Jean Raddon's cat. Night calls for a professional midwife are fairly frequent but it is not often that a cat seeks refuge in such a way! She jumped on to Betty's bed, who hastily evacuated her to the bathroom, and the expectant mother seemed very excited and worried. The midwife remained calm until the first kitten started to arrive and then suddenly realised she did not know what to do and could not even comfort the distressed mother-to-be. However, three kittens safely arrived and Penny seemed no worse for the experience. On Friday, 14th, the situation deteriorated still further. News came through that Hector McMillan's truck had been sequestrated, and a report from Bumba saying that the Baptist Missionary Society missionaries and also Catholic nuns had evacuated from Basoko.

On the next day they received news that soldiers were coming for their truck so they sent a message to Mr. Charles Mann with a house boy, but he was stopped on the road and his bicycle taken by the Simbas and he was sent back to the station. To make matters worse poor Bruce Scholten fell into a nest of driver ants and was badly bitten. On Sunday, worship was maintained and it was Betty's turn to lead the evening fellowship. She earnestly sought the Lord for a message to encourage the hearts of all, and she spoke that night on "God's emergency men — there are no emergencies with God". On Tuesday, 18th August, a group of National Army Soldiers came for the station car, so Bill Scholten went with them in an attempt to keep the vehicle and bring it back again. The hours of daylight wore away and still Bill had not returned. Anxiety increased and then the Lord gave Pearl Hiles Psalm 121, v. 8: "The Lord shall preserve thy going out and thy coming in from this time forth and even for evermore". At 11 o'clock Bill returned by a back road. The next day they found that someone had tried to break into the maternity hospital to remove beds and other furnishings, and also an effort to rob the book store had been made. Then Bill became unwell, suffering from a lump on his head and also went down with filaria. The week closed on the 23rd August by hearing that Volker and Elsie Gscheidle were safe at Wanie Rukulu. It was announced in the Ekoko church that it was unwise to shelter anyone. The next day the Ekoko people experienced a real trial and saw their houseboy nearly murdered in front of their eyes. A group of young children arrived on the mission station dressed mainly in palm leaves and asked Bill to take them to Bumba so that they could join

in the fight. Bill told them that he could not take children
to war. Then they asked the station evangelist to drive them
but Bill again intervened and said that a mission car could
not be used for fighting in any way whatsoever. They went
away a while but returned about 5 p.m. in a vehicle and came
to a halt outside the house of another missionary who was
on furlough. The horn of the vehicle blared continually
until Bill Scholten went up to see what they wanted. A most
objectionable Simba "captain" together with another soldier
and a child of about ten were seeking the "captain's brother
who was a village evangelist". Bill could not help them.
However, they were determined to track the man down
and on hearing that the road was bad and knowing that they
were inexperienced drivers, they ordered Bill to go with them.
Then they forced their way into the house. Mrs. Scholten
signalled Betty to take the children into the bedroom while
the Simbas opened her refrigerator and cleared it of food.
Then they turned and asked the houseboy for a knife. He
hesitated a second, which again angered the soldiers. First
they beat him and then tied him to the bumper of their car.
When Bill and the soldiers left, the terrified boy was crying
for mercy and the "captain" ordered his Simba colleagues
to spear his eyes. Bill pleaded for him and he was released.
But in order to show his power he shot at Bill, singeing his
hair, and threatened to kill him with the next bullet. Bill,
already weakened by prolonged malaria, got into the driver's
cab and went off to seek the brother of the "captain". They
drove for miles on roads with a scrubbing board surface and
Bill did not get back to Ekoko until 4 a.m. on the next day.
Again they received frequent visits from the Simbas. Once
they were all ordered outside their house to be photographed
and while the "captain" was taking pictures the soldier held
his gun a few inches from Betty O'Neill's head. Then came
a sudden change of heart. The "captain" apologised for
making Bill drive so far, saying that he did not know he had
been ill, and the soldier who had stolen Betty's radio gave
her some chickens. It proved to be a bad bargain, for the

previous owner of the chickens — from whom the soldier had
acquired them — demanded them back as he had not received
enough for them! Although the transmitter had now been
confiscated they had managed to keep one radio and they
heard on the news bulletin on the B.B.C. London that there
was a "growing concern for missionaries in N.E. Congo".
Then came further news on the *Voice of America* programme
that the missionaries had been evacuated from Stanleyville
and later that the rebels had refused a Red Cross plane
permission to land.

On Saturday 5th September the Simbas came for the station
truck and its loss nearly broke their hearts as they were
now immobile and quite powerless to move. However, the
work continued! One of the faithful Christians, named Nester,
brought his wife into the maternity hospital on the 6th September with a prayer that she would have a son on this occasion.
They already had three girls. Betty prepared for the delivery
while Nester waited patiently outside. She prepared careful
words to break the news to the anxious father to meet either
eventuality. What a joy it was to her to see a boy come into
the world, but then when she examined the child more closely
she noticed it had six fingers on each hand. The doctor's
services were unavailable and delay could be fatal so she tied
off the extra fingers. After telling Nester the news she was
faced with yet another problem. A patient who had experienced
complications throughout pregnancy — and greater difficulties
during labour — brought forth her baby and almost at the same
time news arrived that the Simbas had killed her husband.
However carefully her words were chosen they seemed inadequate. Sunday, 13th September, was a black day. Bill
Scholten was ill suffering from both fever and diarrhoea.
Pastor Jerome spoke on the need for prayer for the missionaries and at dinner time two truck loads of armed Simbas
arrived and surrounded the Scholten's house. Everyone was
roughly ordered out and one of them pushed Pearl Hiles with
the butt of his gun. They were told they were all going to be
shot and were ordered to take off their shoes and socks and

sit on the sand. Then an argument broke out among the Simbas and Bill was instructed to collect some priests. He went off and the execution of the remainder never took place. Bill returned to the station late that night but went off almost straight away with the Simbas, still endeavouring to protect as much mission property as possible. They waited for over a week for news. Meanwhile some of the children and Pearl Hiles became unwell and it was not until Saturday, 19th September, that they heard Bill was still in Aketi and in prison. On September 22nd, about 9.30 at night, three loyal Congolese came in with a letter from Charles Mann. Betty hastily opened it and read with horror that Bill went to be with the Lord on 16th September. The news came as a great shock and Betty and Pearl went to tell Mrs. Scholten. She took it bravely, knowing that her loved one had suffered much, first with malaria, then on those long enforced drives on forest roads, and then he was beaten severely on the charge of being an American spy.

William Henry Scholten was born in Kalamazoo, Michigan, U.S.A. in 1931 and studied at the Columbia Bible College, South Carolina and the East Tenessee State College. He served the Lord in Belgium for three years, first studying French and designing tracts and Christian publications with a very active tract club in Belgium. While on the continent he carried out a vast survey of France and laid the foundations for the merging of the Alpine Mission in the Ain and Savoy valleys of south France with the Unevangelized Fields Mission. Arriving in Congo in 1962 he taught in the teachers' training school at Ekoko and began an outstandingly successful youth work, one phase of which was a troop of 50 fully trained and uniformed boys under the Flambeaux Movement (Torches). Tents and fishing equipment had been obtained to attract boys to the extensive Christian training course which Bill so enthusiastically gave them. Weekends given to youth work were the joy of his missionary service and he was a man of many capabilities.

A short time after the news was received William "Ike" Scholten, aged 7, woke up and began coughing. Mrs. Scholten went to tend him. She comforted him and then began to break the news to Ike.

"There is something I want to tell you," she began bravely. The little lad looked up and said, "Yes, I know, Mummy. Daddy's gone to be with Jesus."

A Congolese woman had told him that afternoon and, thinking his mother did not want to tell him, he had gone to bed without saying a word. Five days later was Ike's eighth birthday. Just before dinner three truck-loads of Simbas arrived and set up a barrier around the station. They searched and ransacked several houses and the children were terrified. Once they came to their room and announced that they were going to eat some of the children, and later one said he wanted to marry Robbin (aged 7). Poor Ike had no party. There was no cake, there were no games, there were no presents. Just a special kiss from Mummy when she put him to bed.

CHAPTER FOUR

CONFINED TO BARRACKS

As THE BARRIERS CLOSED towards the end of July, a remarkable number of God's servants were, for one reason or another, out of the territory. Mr. and Mrs. D. Muchmore and their two boys, and Mr. and Mrs. W. Snyder and their three children had gone home to the U.S.A. for furlough, Miss Joan Pengilly and Mr. William Gilvear had been called home to attend parents who were dangerously ill and Miss Jean Raddon was on furlough. Mr. and Mrs. Herbert Harms and Mr. and Mrs. C. Sigg and family were at Rethy and could easily cross the Uganda border. Mr. Marshall Southard and Miss Sue Schmit were in Leopoldville, the former returning from a conference, and the latter visiting her brother, while the Director of the Agricultural School near Banjawadi offered a free flight home to Mr. and Mrs. Barrie Morris for the summer vacation. But 67 U.F.M. missionaries and children were trapped.

Just outside the city of Stanleyville stands the impressive headquarters where nearly all the missionaries stayed at one time or another.

The H.Q. building was originally purchased as a children's home but as the children had subsequently transferred their education to the Africa Inland Mission Home and School at Rethy, the building was converted into an administrative H.Q. and a hostel for those passing through Stanleyville. Every missionary had, at some time or another, been accommodated at "Kilometre 8" and had shared in the rich fellowship created by the ministry of Al Larson and the loving hospitality of his wife, Jean.

In this building were staying Rev. and Mrs. Larson and their two-year-old daughter Carol; Mr. and Mrs. Robert McAllister and their three children, who were trapped in

Stanleyville having left their station at Ponthierville for a
shopping expedition; Rev. and Mrs. H. McMillan and their
six children; Mr. and Mrs. C. Davies and two children, who
are missionaries from the Africa Inland Mission and were
serving at the Banjwadi Bible Institute; Mrs. M. Southard
and her son, Larry; the Misses J. Erskine, V. Walker, O.
Bjerkseth, and Mr. and Mrs. D. Carper and their daughter
Caroline.

At first the missionaries continued with their work un-
hindered, travelling around without too many restrictions
and preaching and distributing literature. But as the battle
intensified so pressures against them increased. Groups of
Simbas became regular visitors to the H.Q. and sometimes
demanded food, petrol, money, vehicles or transmitters.
At first the "Regime of Gentlemen" were loyal to their ethical
code of no stealing. One afternoon a truck stopped and a
crowd of young Simbas entered the mission compound.
Hector McMillan and Bob McAllister went to meet them and
were addressed by the leader, probably about 14 years old,
who demanded "Two chickens, immediately". Bob, knowing
of their high standard, instantly replied, "I have no chickens".
Whereupon the Simba looked him straight in the eyes and
replied scathingly, "You are lying". Again Bob emphasised
the truth of the situation. "I had some chickens, but I have
left them all at Ponthierville where I live." The Simba knew
he was avoiding the issue and turned to his followers and
ordered in a coarse voice, "Lions, beat him up". However,
the lions suddenly became chicken-hearted and did not
move towards the 5 feet 8 inch and 15 stone missionary, so
the order was repeated, "Give us two chickens". Again
Bob replied, "I do not have any chickens to give". Unfortunately, at this instant a lone chicken wandered into sight
and began pecking between the stones for food.

The Simba leader looked triumphant. "But there *is* a
chicken in your garden and you are lying to us."

Bob, still emphasising the ethics of the case, replied, "It
is not mine", which infuriated the Simba, who demanded,

"Then who owns it?" Bob McAllister pleaded ignorance. Meanwhile, the remainder of the Simbas who were obviously trying to obey their rules, were getting impatient for a bowl of chicken soup and they set about chasing the innocent creature. The wee white feathered creature gave them a good run for their efforts and after avoiding capture several times was eventually run to ground and picked up. That presented the Simbas with a problem; it ought to be given to the Cause by a white man and not stolen! Billy McAllister, aged 12, was becoming more and more inquisitive and creeping towards his father to hear what was going on. The Simbas saw him and gave the chicken to him. "Go and put it on the truck," they ordered! Whereupon Billy walked out of the compound and placed the frightened bird on the truck waiting in the roadway. His father watched in horror while the ladies watched from the windows of the house to see the next move. They all anticipated that they would order Billy to get on the truck as well. Fortunately, they did not, and they drove off with their prize.

Sometimes the rebels came to carry out house inspections and after two weeks a very tough group arrived to carry out such an inspection. Some of the younger members were obviously awaiting an opportunity to shed the white man's blood and were dangerously fingering the triggers of their guns. The courteous attention which they received did not warrant any such treatment, so after the inspection they were escorted to the grounds, whereupon one raised his gun to his shoulder and fired into the air screaming as he did so. David McAllister, aged ten, was playing around the side of the house and, on hearing the firing, rushed to the feet of the "lions" to collect the spent cartridge cases for souvenirs. Amidst screams, shouts and threats from his parents David manoeuvred his way in between the legs of the soldiers to complete his collection. On another occasion a group of rebels came sauntering into the compound and several of the men went to meet them.

"We want some meat," started the rebel leader.

"Meat," replied Bob McAllister, "Look at all these villages around here. There is no meat anywhere. Your fellow soldiers have come from Stanleyville and have collected all the food for miles around."

The rebel looked dejected and crestfallen, "But we have only rice, and rice without meat is no good."

Bob's face lit up and, with a forced note of surprise, he replied, "Rice? You mean to say you have rice? I only wish we had rice."

Whereupon the rebel, looking now very sorry and rather broken, queried, "Have you no rice, Bwana?"

"Well," replied Bob truthfully, "we have just a little left but we need much more to feed our large family".

The rebel stroked his chin as though in deep thought and, touched with pangs of pity, said, "Ah, Bwana, if ever I meet you in Stanleyville I will give you some rice." Then the angry lions left like lambs!

Although the schools had broken up and the children were on holiday, they found the confines of the garden at H.Q. depressing and the tension under which their parents were living made them restless and irritable. For the first few days they amused themselves by playing hoops with old car tyres, and Mr. Larson managed to obtain a couple of bicycles for them. But all the time the worried parents had to keep a strict eye on them and it seemed as if they were constantly correcting them, "You must not chase chickens, you must not collect cartridge cases, you must keep quiet while the rebels are here, you must not get in the way of the rebels, you must not go near the rebels' vehicles", and so on. After the youngsters had retired one night, the missionaries went to prayer, followed by a time of discussion, and decided that the best thing to do would be to organise routine day classes. Mrs. Lois Carper and Miss V. Walker taught a normal school programme from 8.30 - 12 o'clock and again from 1.30 - 3.30 while Miss Olive Bjerkseth assisted by giving French lessons, thus keeping their minds occupied. Mrs. McMillan ably organised a kindergarten for the younger

" Jeunesse " (Simba Youth) join the show of strength.

After the witchdoctor at Maganga was converted, he publicly burned his fetishes and charms and other symbols of witchcraft.

Prior to evacuation, the Mission cared for hundreds of leprosy patients, and provided them not only with treatment but also with clothing, and sometimes accommodation.

Simbas on the march at Stanleyville.

*The Rebel Leaders (from left to right) : The Military attaché of Gbenge ;
Christophe Gbenge ; Gaston Soumialot ; Nicolas Olenga ;
The Head of Jeunesse, M. Benanga.*

children. Food was becoming short and the men sometimes had to make trips into Stanleyville and as day succeeded day so the tension increased. One evening little Larry Southard, aged 4, kneeling beside his mother to say his prayers said, "Please, Jesus, take the Simbas away on a long, long trip into the forest so that they won't find their way back again."

The presence of midwives at Kilometre 8 soon became known and Mrs. McAllister and Miss Mina Erskine were called upon six times to deliver babies in local villages and had to cycle both ways. The women's meeting, held in the house of one of the believers, continued and during this period Miss Erskine had the privilege of leading one to the Lord. The missionaries felt they should do something for the youngsters, so they began a Bible class for teenage girls which built up to an attendance of 14, while the men occupied themselves in making an additional room for guests from an old hangar frame, which project had been in abeyance for several months. Still the persistent visits of groups of Simbas continued.

One night, a party walked uninvited into the house looking very fierce, and Bob McAllister immediately got up to meet them. Before they had time to demand anything he went to the leader and, smiling pleasantly, he asked, "Do you happen to come from Ponthierville?"

Immediately the face of the rebel also broke into a smile and he almost began purring. "Yes, I do".

"Well, now, isn't that great?" replied Bob extending his hand. "I am the Protestant missionary from Ponthierville."

Whereupon the rebel turned to his colleagues and said, "These are very good people. This is the missionary from Ponthierville. Let us go and leave them alone."

Bob escorted them to the door asking his 'old friend', "And when were you last in Ponthierville?"

The rebel replied, still pleasantly, "Twelve years ago."

It was a happy conversation for Bob and the missionaries, for he had only worked at Ponthierville for the previous eighteen months!

On another occasion the Simbas arrived and arrested all the men, but subsequently released Bob McAllister as he was a "Britisher", whereupon he immediately pleaded for Hector McMillan who, he stated, was also British as he came from Canada. It took some little while to explain where Canada was and its distinction from America but they were eventually satisfied. So Bob and Hector made their way back to Kilometre 8. They had no sooner recounted their story when yet another truckload of rebels arrived, this time demanding a vehicle. It was already dark and Bob replied, "You already have my car. It is a Land Rover and you'll see it in Stanleyville any time you care to look for it."

But the rebel would not be put off. "I need another car."

"But you already have mine," said Bob.

The Simba's patience was exhausted and he turned to his comrades and ordered, "Open that garage, Lions! Burst open that door". At this command a schoolboy 'lion' charged at the door but before he could damage either the door or himself, Bob walked quietly over and said, "Hold on there, lad, and I will open the door with the key. Now, what is your rank and name?"

The youngster replied, "Major John".

"Very well then, Major," replied the missionary, "You only get this car when you write a letter and accept full responsibility for this car as it is not mission property but is owned by a man in Stanleyville."

With some difficulty the letter was written and as Major John entered the cab on the driver's side, Bob opened the other door, shone his torch right in the Simba's face to dazzle him while his left hand reached up and removed the car identity card from the grip on the roof.

"Where is the driver?" demanded Major John. No driver came forward, causing the Major to alter his plans. Another old car was to be abandoned while the driver got in the missionary's vehicle. As the driver's hand went to the ignition key Bob remarked, "Major, just a word before you go. Did you realise that this truck has no lights?"

"What, no lights?" re-echoed the rebel. "In that case we'll have to follow another truck and use those lights."

But Bob McAllister was not beaten! "But, Major, just another word before you go. This truck has very bad brakes and you may end up in the ditch."

"Impossible, impossible, can't go, can't go," stamped the leader of the kings of the jungle — and they went off without a vehicle.

Meanwhile tension was mounting. The children sensed the danger but concentrated on their lessons as much as they were able. Mr. Latham, a United Nations official, invited them to his home which was about one and a half miles away. There they inspected his model railway and this led to a big interest in model making. He gave the boys several "do-it-yourself" model kits and they began constructing a complete model village, including a church, garage, railway and many houses. Aeroplanes, cars and parachutes were also manufactured by the score and McMillan's skill played a big part in shaping the recreation of all the youngsters. He supervised the making of an electric motor and powered it from a six volt car battery and showed the others how to use tools and make reading lamps for their bedrooms. Bulbs were salvaged from a scrapped Volkswagen and the lamps were powered with torch batteries. The tiny tots spent some time in sorting old Christmas cards and on Saturday evenings the children had a games evening when they played Snakes and Ladders, Sorry, Table Football, Chinese Chequers, as well as having some written games and Bible quizzes. Hector McMillan, who was always full of humour, managed to lighten the atmosphere and create some laughs. While the adults were having a session of prayer and the children were

playing happily on one occasion, the elder boys slipped
quietly away. The adults were alarmed to find them missing
and the younger children denied any knowledge of their
whereabouts. They had been instructed firmly enough not
to go outside and not to make a noise. Wherever could they
be? Anxious parents carried out a systematic search of the
house only to find them lying on their backs on the roof
gazing up at the full moon and star-studded skies! It transpired that the lads were following yet another of Hector's
ideas and it was in fact he that organised the 'sky gaze'!

As October days gave way to November so the tension
increased. Al Larson, Del Carper and Charles Davies (A.I.M.)
were arrested and did not return to their families. They were
imprisoned in the Chutes Hotel. Mr. McAllister and Mr.
McMillan were also arrested but were later released when
they proved that they were not Americans! Meanwhile
Mr. Gscheidle willingly went to Kilometre 8 to safeguard
the ladies. Visits from the Simbas became more frequent
and they were noticeably more abusive and demanding.
First they wanted money, then petrol, then food, sometimes
they searched the premises for cameras, typewriters, tape
recorders or transmitters. Gradually the missionaries were
stripped of everything of value. Little did the Simbas know
that hidden away in a cavity in one of the walls were two
large barrels of kerosene and thousands of francs representing
teachers' salaries. They managed to hold on to two trucks
until the last. Then the rebels came and uncompromisingly
demanded Miss Viola Walker's Opel car. It had no radiator
in it so the rebels hauled it away with a Land Rover. On
23rd November they came back for the last truck. It belonged
to Del Carper, was almost new, and had been fitted with
seats to transport the U.F.M. children to and from their
school at Rethy. The loss of this last vehicle was a loss indeed.
It made the missionaries quite immobile and they were
reluctant to let it go. Several times arguing had succeeded
during the course of the 'occupation' but now the rebels
were determined. As Major John ordered his 13-year-old

rebel driver to get into the driving seat, Bob McAllister
went up to him and, standing a few feet away from his rifle,
said, "Major, I want to pray before this truck leaves the
mission. This is number seventeen which you have taken
from us and it is the last one we have. You are leaving us
on our feet to try to carry on God's work of preaching,
education and medical work over a tremendously wide area".

The major stood motionless as Bob closed his eyes and
lowered his head and began to pray, asking that God would
bring back the truck in good condition. Suddenly the young
"lion" interrupted the prayer and asked Bob to pray that he
would not be killed in the fighting. The subject of the prayer
altered. Bob prayed God's protection on this young, mis-
guided man and asked that he might have his eyes opened
and that he might come to a knowledge of the Truth. Only
ten minutes before, he had been threatening to shoot Bob
and as he opened his eyes he saw that the head of the Simba
had also been bowed in prayer.

Everyone was very uneasy when they went to bed that night
and they knew that the situation could not last much longer.
Something would have to happen, but little did they know that
the following day was going to be the most dramatic in their
lives and that one of their number would be summoned to
Higher Service.

CHAPTER FIVE

THE MIRACULOUS DELIVERANCE

"THE LORD stood with me and strengthened me, that by me the preaching might be fully known, and that all the Gentiles might hear: and I was delivered out of the mouth of the lion" (II Timothy 4, v. 17). So wrote the Apostle Paul while lying in prison awaiting execution, as he reflected on a miraculous deliverance in the past. The situation in which Al Larson and Del Carper found themselves was strangely similar.

On the morning of the 24th November, 1964, the hostages held in the Victoria Hotel, Stanleyville, were awakened by the drone of aeroplanes overhead. It had just gone six o'clock and the first sign of dawn appeared on the horizon. The drone of aeroplanes was ominous. Alfred Larson raised himself on his elbow from his resting place on the floor and nudged Del Carper who was lying beside him. "If those aeroplanes have not got paratroopers on them we are as good as dead men," he said. His assessment of the reaction of the Simbas was deadly accurate, but the fact that a day of unprecedented action was about to commence was unforeseen although everyone hastily got up and dressed. Al looked out of the window. The aeroplanes were flying in accurate formation and were passing right over the city, no doubt on their way to the airfield. As the clock struck eight a large party of Simbas arrived at the door of the hotel shouting and gesticulating wildly. The hostages were ordered outside into the street and everyone knew that the Simbas would carry out their threats and kill those in their clutches. It was a battle for time — one in which seconds mattered. They delayed as long as possible, collecting boots, doing up their shoes and crowding the doorways. But eventually they were lined up in threes and told to march down the road. There were just

over 250 in the party in total, including Al Larson and Del
Carper (both of U.F.M.), Charles Davies (a young missionary
with the Africa Inland Mission), Dr. Paul Carlson (of the
Mission Evangelique Ubangi), Miss Phyllis Rine (of the
African Christian Mission) the American and Belgian consular
staffs and many Belgian men, women and children. They
began a forced march down the road guarded by Simbas on all
sides carrying their sten guns, ready to shoot at any minute.
They thought at first that they would be taken to the Lumumba
Square where untold hundreds of Congolese had been executed
during the four months' reign of the Populaire Government.
The official executioner was just ten years old and during those
months he had taken over 50 lives. At the side of the Square
was mounted a huge painting of the deceased hero-leader,
Lumumba, encased in a stone surround and set upon a flight
of steps. Time after time those who opposed the new *regime*
were sacrificed before the blood-stained monument. But
the procession by-passed the road leading to Lumumba
Square, leaving it two blocks away on their left, and was
led to a plot of waste ground in the same road as the hotel.
The human caterpillar was halted half-way round a corner
leaving it roughly in the shape of an 'L'.

One of the rebel leaders, named Opepe and self-styled as
"colonel", walked up and down in front of them and made
his last speech. Opepe was not in full agreement with many
of the practices of the rebels and had genuinely done all
that he could to make the position of the white hostages as
easy as possible. "For over four months I have looked after
you white people. I have cared for you and protected you,
but now your brothers are interfering in our struggle for liberty
and I can be no longer responsible for what happens to you".
As he was speaking a group of Simbas unloaded a machine
gun from a lorry and mounted it in front of the unfortunate
captives. In the distance they heard the sound of shooting
and knew that rescue was only minutes away. Still the
"colonel" continued with a rambling speech but by this time
the obvious intentions of the rebels absorbed the concentration

of the hostages and no one heard what he was saying. An argument broke out among the Simbas as to who was to do the shooting, as they pointed the ugly muzzle of the gun toward the captives. Again and again the sound of shouts lfiled the air. The Simbas, realising that time was running out, abandoned the use of their machine gun. Suddenly one opened fire with his sten gun and immediately 20-30 others pulled their triggers, spraying the line with hot lead. Immediately the street was turned into a scene of confusion. Added to the noise of the guns rose shouts, cries and screams as people scattered in all directions. The group of four missionaries squatting on the extreme wing of the line fell to the ground. As the first round of gunfire ceased and the Simbas were reloading, Al Larson, Charles Davies and Paul Carlson made a dash for their lives. Del Carper, who had been deprived of his hearing aid by the Simbas as they thought it was a transmitter and he was speaking to his comrades, was unable to hear what was going on, so he laid beside two dead bodies feigning death. Two or three times the missionaries fell to the ground as bullets were fired in their direction as they raced towards a group of houses about fifteen yards away on the other side of the road. It was the custom of the Belgians to build a small sun-parlour without a roof in the front of their homes which also served as a porchway. Al Larson and Charles Davies dived over the wall of the nearest sun-parlour and Charles reached over the top of the wall to help up Paul Carlson. There was another burst of gunfire and Charles Davies felt Carlson's body go limp. He let go of his hands and Carlson slumped to the ground, having been shot five times in the back and once in the head. Three Belgians managed to get over the same porchway and then a Belgian couple raced toward the same place of refuge carrying their two children. A Simba ran to a tree less than twenty-five yards away and levelled his gun toward them. The couple, a Mr. and Mrs. Paneff, threw over one child, who landed in Al's arms, before the Simba opened fire and they were both wounded. Mrs. Paneff, whom the men in prison

had called "Florence Nightingale" because of her good care
and cheerful disposition, was alive, but had three bullets
in her body. Her husband was also injured. The other child,
also slightly wounded, escaped death and as the round of
ammunition came to an end she ran off screaming only yards
from the one who had tried to take her life. As the Simba
was reloading his gun, Al Larson went to the door and tried
to open it. Summoning every ounce of strength possible he
put his foot to the door, which yielded under the impact.
In the living room a frightened Belgian woman was clutching
her little girl, crying, "Ma petite, ma petite". Al looked
around the house for refuge and spotted a large cupboard
under the stairs. He went in, followed by the rest of the party,
and called to the woman to come in with them. She refused,
believing that she was safer where she was. Outside a battle
was taking place, and minutes later two Simbas entered the
house seeking the escapees. Breathlessly the group waited
in silence. They heard two shots. The Simbas turned over
the furniture, tore down the curtains, opened every cupboard,
except the one where the missionaries and Belgians were
hiding. The sound of shouting increased and it was obvious
that the Belgian paratroopers had arrived. Using bazookas
and grenades, and throwing a rain of lead, they raced down
the road toward the centre of the scene of massacre. The
streets were lined with bodies, thirty-five dead, many more
wounded and some feigning death. The Simbas fled as the
troops entered the road. Al Larson heard his name
being called and left his hiding place. It was a
miraculous escape. He and his colleagues had been delivered
out of the mouth of the lions. If the little girl whom he was
still holding had cried or even whimpered, their hiding place
would have been betrayed and all would have been lost.
It was a tremendous relief to him to see Del Carper walking
towards the house quite uninjured, although shaken.

Al sought out the Belgian commander and asked him to
send a relief party to the headquarters which stood just five
miles outside the town. After Al had found the Belgian

commander he could not persuade him to make the journey
to Kilometre 8.   The commander was under strict orders
that his men must not move beyond the perimeter of the city
itself and he dared not order the relief of Kilometre 8 in spite
of the fact that nine women, two men and fourteen children
were held there. The mercenaries, who should have arrived
at Stanleyville at the same time as the parachute drop, had
met fierce opposition on the way and several road blocks.
They did not arrive until 10 o'clock that morning.

Meanwhile Al investigated the fate of other U.F.M.
missionaries in the city. David and Sonia Grant had been
imprisoned in a Roman Catholic hostel nearby.   Mr. and
Mrs. Grant were stationed at Banjwadi, but one afternoon
late in October rebels had arrived and had taken the Grants
and Mr. and Mrs. Davies to Stanleyville, which was sixty-four
kilometres away. They did not know the purpose of the trip
and as the lorries stopped at roadblocks on the way they were
constantly tormented by threats. David Grant (the brother
of Beryl Grant, the secretary and organist of the People's
Gospel Hour), was in one truck and his wife, Sonia, in
another. Sonia covered her head with a towel and prayed
throughout the journey. As the Simbas crowded round the
truck to jeer at their captives, Sonia quoted aloud for the
benefit of her white colleagues a passage from Psalm 27
which she had been reading that very afternoon: "Though
an host should encamp against me my heart shall not fear.
Though wars should rise against me in this I will be confident".
Strangely enough, the Simbas listened too, so Sonia continued
with the familiar words of John 3, v. 16: "God so loved the
world that He gave His only begotten Son that whosoever
believeth in Him should not perish but have everlasting life".
Then she gave her testimony and told the story which she
had repeated so many times in Congo of Christ's love for
all men. Some of the Simbas remarked, "She isn't frightened".
The rebel "colonel" ordered that this group of hostages be
imprisoned in the Catholic Mission. Both David and Sonia
are adamant Protestants strongly opposed to the errors of

Romanism, yet by some strange coincidence they were separated from their missionary brethren and put under arrest with a large party of Roman Catholics with whom they were forced to live for four weeks! All hostages in the Roman Catholic Mission were rescued without injury. Similarly, a group of five missionaries who had been cut off in the literature shop and store room were also released, and their story is recorded in a separate chapter.

When the mercenaries arrived they were battle weary, hungry and thirsty, but Al presented to them the urgent need of the group at Kilometre 8. A party agreed to make a sortie to rescue Rev. and Mrs. H. McMillan and their six sons; Mr. and Mrs. R. McAllister and their three children; Mrs. T. Southard and her son Larry, aged 4; Mrs. Charles Davies and two children; Mrs. Carper and one child; Mrs. Larson and baby Carol, aged 2, along with Miss Olive Bjerkseth, Miss Viola Walker and Miss Mina Erskine. Al Larson and David Grant climbed on the back of two of the vehicles and Al directed the mercenaries towards their destination. There was very little opposition on the way, although the men fired periodically at the sight of a Congolese and Al had to plead for the lives of several Africans whom he recognised and knew that they were not sympathetic to the rebel movement. It was just past eleven o'clock when the armoured cars arrived at H.Q. and as Al jumped from the jeep he sensed that something was wrong. Half crawling and half running he made his way towards the house, believing that it had been captured by the Simbas and expecting any minute a burst of gunfire from one of the windows. Suddenly the door opened and out came Bob McAllister to greet Al.

"Are there any Mulelists about?" he asked. Rebels were alternatively known as Mulelists from the name of one of their early leaders in Lower Congo.

"Not one," replied Bob. And then he broke the sad news that Hector had gone to be with the Lord.

CHAPTER SIX

ONE MURDER AND FOUR MIRACLES

ALMOST AS SOON as the paratroopers dropped, the infuriated Simbas made their way towards Kilometre 8. Two jeep-loads arrived and roughly ordered everyone outside. By their attitude the missionaries knew that something was wrong and they, too, had heard the aircraft going overhead in the early hours of the morning, though they had not seen the parachute drop. They accused the missionaries of transmitting to the aircraft. Suddenly Mr. McAllister realised that the engine of their water pump, which was switched on for two hours every morning to pump sufficient fresh water into the house for their daily need, was still throbbing and the Simbas thought it was a transmitter. He explained to them the purpose of the pump but they refused to accept it. Obligingly Mr. McMillan switched it off. Then the missionaries were ordered back inside their home again while the Simbas engaged in a fierce argument outside. Then one of the soldiers called to them and ordered them outside again and they were lined up in front of the little stone wall while soldiers loaded their guns. Fearfully they watched and realised only too well that this was to be the end. It was the intention of the Simbas to kill every one of them.

To say that another miracle took place is no exaggeration. In answer to the thousands of prayers ascending on behalf of those in Congo from all over the world God intervened at this moment of crisis. The Simbas decided to take away the two men, Rev. H. McMillan and Mr. R. McAllister, whilst the women and children were ordered back inside the living room. Silently, they filed back into their room, their hearts burdened with grief for the two fathers, and began sitting on the chairs. As the last one entered the room, one of the Simbas put his sten-gun through the doorway and opened fire. Instinctively the women fell to the ground, clutching the children and lying on top of them. Again the hand of God covered them as not one of the children screamed or cried, even baby Carol put her little hands over her ears and lay perfectly still. The Simba, believing his bloody task was done, turned from the room. However, the two men, on hearing the firing, stopped in their tracks, whereupon one of the Simbas opened fire on them. Rev. Hector McMillan was killed instantly, being shot several times through the back. Bob McAllister turned around stunned, scarcely realising that the voice of his colleague had been silenced.

"You, you have killed my brother," he stammered, where upon the same gun was turned upon him. The shot passed so close to his forehead that it stunned him and he fell to the ground and lay motionless for some ten minutes while the Simbas made off in their vehicles.

Stanleyville was in an uproar. Cars passed by and one or two Africans saw the two missionaries lying outside their headquarters and passed round the news that they were both dead. Mrs. McAllister and Mrs. Southard came out of the headquarters and hastily examined the body of Hector McMillan, soon realising that he was now beyond human aid. They rushed to Mr. McAllister shouting, "Bob, are you all right?"

What a relief for his dear wife when he opened his eyes and answered "Yes".

They carried Hector's body inside the house and laid it on a bed. Bob then looked around and saw two of the McMillan boys receiving first-aid treatment. Kenny, aged 17, had been shot in the thigh, and a splinter of a bullet had hit Paul McMillan, aged 16, in the cheek. Although wounded, these two boys had lain quite silently until the Simba had fled. They were treated and the next two hours were extremely anxious. At any time the Simbas might return. Their actions were irresponsible and unpredictable and still the missionaries were not positive that rescue was on the way. After hasty consultation they decided to make some sandwiches and take the children into the forest and be prepared to stop there all night. Bob McAllister took his saw and cut some boards and made a crude coffin for Hector, hoping the Africans would bury the body in the grounds of the headquarters where Hector had been the first house father for the missionaries' children.

Hector McMillan was loved by all the missionaries. He was essentially a handyman. On one occasion the electricity generating plant had lain idle for a year waiting for Hector to return from furlough as he was the only man who could repair it. A colleague said of him, "A difficult job is done immediately, and an impossible one takes him a little longer". He earnestly coveted the conversion and call of his six sons and rose very early in the morning to pray for them and to seek a message from God's Word to leave with them at family prayers.

Some were ready to evacuate to the woods, but before leaving the house they knelt in prayer: "O Lord, give us immediate deliverance". Mrs. Ione McMillan called her family around the body of Hector. She knew it would be the last time that they would see him. "Missionary work is a work of sacrifice. Some people are called to give money and some time. You have been called to give your daddy. He was a great and wonderful missionary". The family bowed their heads while the recently widowed Ione led them in prayer. Then Mina Erskine, Jean Larson, Lois Carper and Mrs. Davies took the tiny tots into the woods, with a substantial supply of sandwiches and foodstuffs in case it meant stopping there all night. However, after about two hours they heard the familiar voice of Al Larson ringing through the trees, calling for them. They left their hiding place and saw Al with a party of dishevelled mercenaries waiting at the gates of the headquarters. Although brief, it was a joyful reunion as Al met his wife and his baby daughter for the first time in three weeks.

Salvation had come to Kilometre 8. The vehicles were already heavily loaded with food, water, petrol and ammunition and it seemed impossible to get one additional person on, let alone twenty-four. Having anticipated an evacuation they had their bags packed and they began to pile on the trucks. It proved impossible. "Leave all baggage behind," commanded the mercenary N.C.O. and the missionaries had to leave their suitcases, parcels and packages just where they were and climb onto the relieving trucks. The children lay on the floor, while parents sheltered them with their own bodies. Then began a desperate and hair-raising trip back to Stanleyville. Three times they met road blocks. Several times snipers shot at them and both lorries were hit. And yet another miracle must be recorded, for there was not a single missionary or child injured in that journey to the airport. At the airport they were met by Mr. Del Carper who soon found a stretcher to transport Kenny McMillan. They registered as refugees with the Government official who had erected a temporary table actually on the airfield, and waited for the next aeroplane down to Leopoldville.

So many have spoken of "giving up everything for Christ" and at this point they were faced with stark reality. They had nothing except the clothes in which they stood. Their homes, baggage, equipment and money was all behind, together with the work that they had poured out their lives to establish. Thirty years of prayer and labour was left under the paw of the lion and yet they knew that the gates of hell could not prevail against the Church which had been established.

CHAPTER SEVEN

BUSINESS AS USUAL

As soon as Mr. Herbert Jenkinson was demobbed from the Machine Gun Guards after World War I he went into training for the mission field. He first sailed for Congo in February 1920, and joined a gallant band of pioneers seeking to make known the name of Christ in an area which was completely pagan. He struggled with a native language and soon conquered it, but found that the Congolese could not pronounce his name, nor did it seem that their thick lips would ever allow the name of "Jenkinson" to roll from them freely. The natives therefore omitted the first and last syllables of his name and called him "Kinso", which has remained with him throughout his missionary career. Now, not only the Congolese but fellow missionaries, home staff and prayer supporters alike affectionately refer to this pioneer of the Gospel as "Kinso". His early years were spent in pioneering the Gospel over a wide area. In 1932 he began building the Bongondza station on virgin jungle land and supervised the clearing of the ground and the erection of building after building. In 1935 he was appointed Field Leader and was greatly respected by all for his spiritual counsel and insight. In 1955 he inspired the building of the Banjwadi Bible Institute which was aimed at preparing Congolese nationals to take over all pastoral and administrative duties. It was one of the five seminaries which attained theological college status in Congo and several other Missions co-operated in its administration. Mrs. Alice Jenkinson also sailed for the field in 1920 and has faithfully worked alongside her husband and has specialised in women's work. In 1961 they came home at the request of the Home Council to assist the Rev. L. F.

Left—Mr. Del Carper and Mr. Bill Scholten try out the new radio transmitter which was installed on the 23rd March 1964.

The ward which was abandoned, together with expectant mothers, when the missionaries were arrested.

Below—Two patients who came to Ekoko for treatment. Both had deep knife wounds sustained during the fighting.

Mothers and babies at Ekoko.

The Flambeaux (Torches). Mr. William Scholten gave much time to this movement during his ministry in Congo.

Mr. and Mrs. W. Scholten and their family during the period of house arrest.

Bruce's birthday party on the 24th October 1964

The unmarked mound of earth is Bill Scholten's grave.

Henry, a leprosy sufferer, with his wife and family.

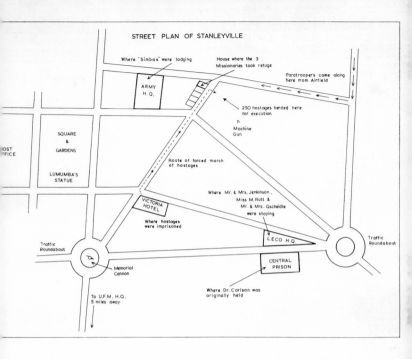

STREET PLAN OF STANLEYVILLE

Where "Simbas" were lodging

House where the 3 Missionaries took refuge

Paratroopers came along here from Airfield

ARMY H.Q.

250 hostages herded here for execution

Machine Gun

SQUARE & GARDENS

POST OFFICE

LUMUMBA'S STATUE

Route of forced march of hostages

Where Mr. & Mrs. Jenkinson, Miss M. Rutt & Mr. & Mrs. Gscheidle were staying

VICTORIA HOTEL

Where hostages were imprisoned

LECO H.Q.

Traffic Roundabout

Traffic Roundabout

Memorial Cannon

CENTRAL PRISON

Where Dr. Carlson was originally held

To U.F.M. H.Q. 5 miles away

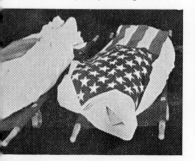

The bodies of Dr. Paul Carlson (MEU) and Miss P. Rine (AMC) awaiting burial.

The first plane load of wounded leaving Stanleyville.

The majority of the U.F.M. Family queueing up to register as ' Refugees ' on the airfield.

Kenny McMillan (17) being carried on a stretcher to the 'plane. He was shot in the leg.

Major Bu-Bu—the rebel leader reputed to have given the order to shoot the hostages on 24/11/64 in Stanleyville. It was his truck which brought the machine gun for the proposed killings.

Harris, the General Secretary, who had been seriously ill. However, on Mr. Harris' recovery the call of Congo persisted and they felt compelled to return to the land which had already claimed the best years of their lives.

Mr. and Mrs. Jenkinson have always kept up with the times and they saw that Christian literature was going to play a vital part in the Congo of the future. The country was rapidly becoming literate and as education increased so the power of the printed page became more vital. They dedicated the remainder of their lives to literature evangelism and after obtaining approval of the Home Council they travelled the country making known their latest project. It took just eighteen months to collect sufficient money to purchase a Bedford Workobus which would act as a travelling showroom and visit the whole of the U.F.M. area. They were seconded to an inter-mission Christian literature project, known as the *Librairie Evangelique au Congo* (L.E.C.O.) and were allocated a large building in the city of Stanleyville which would act as a shop, store room, office and also have room to spare for living accommodation. It was situated in a good central place in town and Miss Mary Rutt, who looked after the accounts, also had an apartment in the building. A large party assembled on Liverpool Street Station to see them off on this latest venture.

The Communists were not unmindful of the power of literature. They had more than 400,000 trained literature agents at work in Southern Asia and Africa and the works of Lenin and Marx and other Communist leaders well exceeded the circulation of Scripture portions. It was estimated that Russia spent £500 million a year on literature, publishing in 175 languages. How truly the Archbishop of York had stated, "Is not this the time to alert the churches, and, beyond the strict limits of the churches, the well disposed public, to the fact which none can deny unless they shut their eyes, that the real battle is being fought in the realm of ideas and that ideas are born and nourished by literature. Nothing less is called for than the impregnation of society at all levels of culture in all races of the world with literature which conveys the Christian message." So, Mr. and Mrs. Jenkinson took up their post in Stanleyville, assisting Rev. and Mrs. Briggs of the B.M.S. who were in charge of the work in the city. They were amazed at the way their books sold. Sometimes they carried Scriptures in as many as twelve languages and, in addition to their ministry as colporteurs, found ample opportunity for Bible teaching. The doors of their shop seldom closed. Sometimes Mrs. Jenkinson would sit in the porchway and enrol students for correspondence courses. They became well known in Stanleyville. They were assisted by Miss Mary Rutt from the U.S.A., who looked after purchasing, recording and accounting.

When the rebellion broke out in July 1964 Mr. and Mrs. Jenkinson and Miss Mary Rutt were trapped in their literature store and shortly afterwards were joined by Mr. and Mrs. Volker Gscheidle, two German workers. This couple had been working at Wanie Rukula when the rebels captured the town, but were later rescued by the gallantry of Mr. Peter Rombaut, the acting British Vice Consul, and brought back to Stanleyville. Later they came to assist the Kinsos at Leco. In spite of the growing pressures against white people and the frequent threats of death, the bookstore remained open. Sometimes the Simbas themselves would come in and buy a Bible or Testament. Frequently Mrs. Jenkinson entertained two or three in the living room and, after giving them a cup of tea, talked about her Saviour. While the crisis was at its height a huge car drove up outside the bookstore and the wife of General Olinga, the rebel leader who eventually ordered the execution of the hostages, alighted, and with her body guards entered the shop. She bought a hymn book.

On another occasion several Simbas visited Mr. and Mrs. Jenkinson and charged them with firing a rifle from their window towards the prison. After some time they were persuaded that the Kinso's did not have a gun and left — but strange as it may seem, Mr. Jenkinson later found a hole in the mosquito netting on the window, about the size of a bullet and with the wire bent outwards — just as though a gun had in fact been fired. The compartment had remained locked during the night and no visitors had been received, so if the Simbas had discovered the hole it might have led to the arrest or even death of the Kinso's. The hole still remains a mystery, for no one can guess how it got there.

Late one night a lady's voice was heard calling from the street, "Mr. Kinso. Mr. Kinso". Who could it be? The strange thing about the call was the "Mr.", for those who knew Mr. Jenkinson intimately invariably omitted the "Mr." and just addressed him as Kinso. When they went down to investigate they found poor Mrs. Davies of the A.I.M. in a state of collapse, for not only had she been transferred from Banjwadi to Stanleyville by the Simbas but also her husband was still under arrest, and being straight from the U.S. had not yet conquered the language. Mrs. Davies and the children had been ill-treated also. At the military camp a man had been shot dead beside them, and they had a terrifying experience. Happily, Mrs. Davies and the children had managed to get to Leco and later they were able to get out to Kilometre 8.

The Simbas impounded the long-awaited and much prayed for Workobus, which confined this party of five missionaries to the boundaries of Stanleyville, but even so Mr. Jenkinson received several invitations to preach in local churches and was actually present at a baptismal service during September. The prison stood immediately opposite the bookstore and it was here that Dr. Paul Carlson and his colleagues were detained. Mrs. Jenkinson, Mrs. Gscheidle and Miss Rutt prepared their meals and did their washing, and Mr. Jenkinson and Mr. Gscheidle frequently took them across to the prison.

Through this ministry of mercy the prisoners managed to keep alive. They sent their clothing across to the Kinso's for laundering with the empty trays, and the shirts were often bloodstained, indicating maltreatment. Atrocities continued, rumours abounded, the atmosphere grew tense, but still the bookshop doors remained open and still the flow

of the Words of Life continued into the centre of the city.
In fact, these doors remained open until November 23rd.
Kinso realised that the end must come soon and they packed
their bags ready for evacuation.

As the parachutes came down and Simbas began running
wildly in every direction, they expected a party to storm up
their stairway at any moment to finish their lives. They could
hear shooting and screaming in the direction of the Army H.Q.
close by, and later saw Simbas slinking away hurriedly. At
about 11 o'clock Belgian paratroopers were seen skirmishing
at the prison across the road. Mr. Gscheidle contacted them
and was informed that all whites were ordered to make their
way to a reception centre in the direction of the airport.

Kinso was reluctant to leave, knowing the extreme danger
of those at Kilometre 8 and at that time not knowing what
had happened to Al Larson or Del Carper. He therefore
remained behind while Mr. Gscheidle conducted his wife,
Mrs. Jenkinson and Miss Rutt to the reception centre. Dead
bodies were lying about as they picked their way along, but
as soon as the Belgian paratroopers saw them, they came to
their aid.

Kinso, realising that it was useless to remain inactive, went
into the street to see what could be done. Belgian paratroopers
asked him to direct them to a spot where they had heard there
were some wounded. The journey took them close to the
Reception Centre where he learned that Al Larson was safe
and had already left for the rescue of those at Kilometre 8.
In a short while the news came that they had arrived at the
airport but that Hector McMillan had been killed. This news
cast a great shadow over the relief and the rescue, but all
realised that the casualties could have been very much heavier.

On arrival home, he received an unexpected letter. It was
from the State Department in Washington:—

"DEAR MR. AND MRS. JENKINSON,

*Speaking for the Government of the United States and on
our own behalf, we in the Bureau of African Affairs wish to
express our warmest appreciation for the aid given by you*

*to our Consular staff in Stanleyville. Never will the five men
forget their amazement and pleasure in finding that immediately after their secret transfer to the Central Prison food was
provided for them by you. They knew then and in the days
and weeks to come that they were not abandoned and forgotten.*

*Your assistance made it possible for our men to endure
their imprisonment and to emerge from it in good physical
and mental condition. Thank you.*

*With every good wish,
Sincerely yours,*

G. MENNEN WILLIAMS".

Kinso is one of God's gentlemen. The Spirit of Christ
radiates from him, and one cannot but feel when talking with
him that here is a man who knows God. And this is the
secret of the wonderful blessing which he has experienced
over his long years on the field. He has forty-five years of
foreign missionary service to his credit and a letter from the
State Department in Washington — yet he has infinitely
more than that, for both at home and abroad are hundreds
who look on him as a spiritual benefactor, and breathe a
prayer of thanksgiving that he passed their way. The gentle,
loving and deeply considerate Ma Kinso too will never be
forgotten in Congo. Her work among the women and children
can never fade away for she 'gave herself to them'. When
one's work is etched on lives with the indelible ink of Christlike love it lasts throughout eternity. Perhaps her own poem
gives a glimpse of her soul that words could never portray.

MARKET DAY

The palms lift their arms giving welcome shade
  In the glare of the morning sun;
An air of expectancy broods over all,
  For the market has begun.
From hidden paths in the jungle around
  Comes the lilt of a happy song,
And in Indian file the folks stream in
  Bringing their wares along.
There's a pageant of colour, a riot of sound,
  A marvellous mixture of smells!
There are laughs and smiles as the seller beguiles,
  With the wonderful tale that he tells.
Look around on the scene: has there ever been
  A more fitting place for the Gospel?
They have come from far, they have come from near,
  Ready for anything they may hear.
So we tell them simply of God's good grace
  And an interest quickens on every face;
They listen and listen and take it in —
  The story of Jesus who saves from sin.
Then back to their forest homes they go,
  With thoughts fresh kindled, and faces aglow.
How happy we'll be when we see His face,
  That we preached His Word in the market place.

ALICE JENKINSON, CONGO.

CHAPTER EIGHT

AKETI DIARY

AFTER THE DEATH of the Rev. W. Scholten, the remainder of the party at Ekoko were arrested and taken to Aketi. After a mock 'trial' they were told they could return to their station, but owing to the long journey for the children, they asked if they could remain at Aketi, lodging with Mr. and Mrs. Charles Mann.

As the Aketi group entered the month of October they began feeling the strain under which they were forced to live. The children became fretful and frequently sick, the adults had aches and pains, the guards were armed with guns as well as machettes. The traffic on the roads increased, tension among the Simbas became greater and reports of aerial bombing and strafings and subsequent atrocities were more frequent. Miss Betty O'Neill faithfully maintained her diary.

OCTOBER 1ST. Interviewed by the rebel "major" who had sent for us. He was dressed in purple, white and yellow pyjamas and carried a gun in one hand and a bottle of beer in the other. After examination we were told we could go back to Ekoko, but Mrs. Scholten asked if we could stay at Mr. and Mrs. Mann's home in Aketi as we were black and blue from the journey. If it were not for the fact that the sky had clouded over we would have been sunburnt as well. How gracious is the Lord!

FRIDAY, 2ND. Everyone suffering from aches and pains. Heard over the radio of bombs and riots in Belfast!

MONDAY, 5TH. Pearl Hiles ill. She bumped her head the day we came to Aketi and is feeling dizzy.

THURSDAY, 8TH. All the children have colds and coughs. Ike has an infected toe.

SATURDAY, 10TH. Letter arrived from Al Larson. All the bush stations have had a hard time. Dotty Scholten ill, Pearl still poorly.

MONDAY, 12TH. Robbin's birthday. I helped Robbin bake her cake but Bruce, Steven and Stephanie Mann all unwell. Pearl a little better. Received some letters from Stanleyville.

WEDNESDAY, 14TH. The "major" visited us again, still wearing his pyjamas.

SUNDAY, 18TH. Cynthia Mann (9 months) fell head first into a bucket of water.

MONDAY, 19TH. A lot of traffic on the road. A Simba came and told us that it is useless to hide from the planes as they come down and blow the grass away!

Steven has a rash so stopped penicillin injections.

TUESDAY, 20TH. Heavy tropical storm. The rain beat into the house.

WEDNESDAY, 21ST. Bruce ill with temperature of 102.5 F. Started him on penicillin and sent a note to the Doctor who was in prison, to come if possible.

THURSDAY, 22ND. Heard from Ferdinand, a Congolese Christian, that a man had been shot at the rail station after having had his ears and nose cut off.

FRIDAY, 23RD. Started Ike on penicillin. Robbin and Dotty have fever, Bruce better.

SATURDAY, 24TH. News of Bill Scholten's death on the *Voice of America* radio programme. It was Bruce's birthday and I helped him make a cake. Had great difficulty in giving Ike his injection. Dotty feeling ill but Robbin a little better. Tried to organise a party for Bruce. The children enjoyed it but got very dirty.

SUNDAY, 25TH. Steven Mann wandered into the church and a Simba brought him home again!

MONDAY, 26TH. A Greek, called George, sent us some biscuits and tea and Jacob (a houseboy) sent us some bread.

TUESDAY, 27TH. I was called at 5 a.m. as Charles Mann became sick. At 5 p.m. a plane came over Aketi strafing and bombing. The poor women were frightened. Bruce just said, "Planes in sky," and went and had his supper! At 11.30 p.m. three Simbas came to take us all to jail. They changed their minds, but arrested Charles Mann. They released him after a while and he came back.

WEDNESDAY, 28TH. Heard that George, the Greek who sent us food, had been beaten to death in jail. In the evening three Simbas came to arrest us. They took us to a house and put us in a room with five nuns and a Belgian woman and her two children. Some had been beaten and molested. We "slept" on the floor.

THURSDAY, 29TH. We got some stale bread which a Portuguese had left and Dotty put some jam on it. When the children had eaten what they wanted we ate the rest.

FRIDAY, 30TH. I asked if I could go to our house for some of our things. The men advised against it but I felt I should go for the children's sake. I went in the back of a truck with Simbas and was away three hours.

SATURDAY, 31ST. Managed to get a bath. A priest offered to say Mass for Bill and George on the following day but Dotty spoke to him and explained that our faith was in the Sacrifice of Christ.

SUNDAY, NOVEMBER 1ST. The Catholics had Mass and we had a service. Had a visit from a "major" who gave men a hard time for not recognising him. Heard that a mother of two little girls had been molested five times and her little girl of five and a half was threatened, but she pleaded and the child was not touched.

MONDAY, 2ND. This was Dotty's birthday and we were up nearly all night with the children. We saw about 1,700 marching and knew that there was to be heavy fighting. Planes flew overhead but no bombs were dropped.

TUESDAY, 3RD. A young Simba told us that two whites had been killed at Banalia. Dr. Jacob saw some of the men who had been in prison. Some could hardly walk and their backs were lacerated from constant beatings. Pearl fell and hurt her knee.

WEDNESDAY, 4TH. Cynthia Mann nearly choked. She cried, held her breath, went stiff and blue and gave us all a fright. Steven Mann developed fever and Pearl had a pain in her chest. A "major" visited us and told us that wives were not to speak to their husbands or we would be tied up.

THURSDAY, 5TH. Simbas came looking for the Doctor, the "nurse" who had been looking after the white men who were beaten. Then they beat him with sticks and pipes and cut his head.

They searched the house looking for radios, stripped the men to their underpants and marched them all to prison. Later Charles Mann and another man came back. In the prison they had beaten the "nurse" again, who had to be carried back into the house.

FRIDAY, 6TH. Visits from Simbas on and off all day. Little Sandy became sick in the night. In the evening news came through that Kindu had fallen to the National army and our guards sharpened their knives on the stones outside the house.

SATURDAY, 7TH. Dotty had a long talk with the other women about Bill and the Lord.

SUNDAY, 8TH. The Catholics had Mass and we had a service. New guards arrived carrying guns.

MONDAY, 9TH. Sandy and I could not sleep owing to cramp. Planes came over and there was shooting and bombing.

THURSDAY, 12TH. Hardly any sleep. Children restless and grown-ups irritable. A "major" came to me and asked me to dress his wound. He showed us a bullet hole in his handker-chief and told us that he had killed 2,000 Americans at Bunduki!

SUNDAY, 15TH. Had a service together. We started a study in Leviticus, chapters 1 and 2. It was the "offering" that was accepted, not the one who offered.

MONDAY, 16TH. Dotty has a pain in her chest. I wonder how much longer we can hold out?

TUESDAY, 17TH. Up at 4 a.m. Some of the nuns are unwell. Two are over 70 years old.

WEDNESDAY, 18TH. Sandy up in night suffering from vomiting and fever and laid about all day. Obtained some stale bread but it tasted good after it was toasted.

THURSDAY, 19TH. A Simba on a bike used a trumpet to summon all Simbas. It seems the fighting is getting nearer.

FRIDAY, 20TH. Wrote to the doctor in prison asking per-mission to go through his drugs and use some. He gave it. In the evening a "major" arrived and we were all ordered outside and lined up. He shouted and raved at us for a while and struck us all four times on the head with his ebony baton. He even hit little Cynthia Mann (9 months) who was cradled in her mother's arms. But she didn't cry, only hid her head in her mother's shoulder. When they discovered I was not an American they sent me into a side room. I said I wanted to stay with Dotty and the "major" did his best to make me understand that I had to make a choice and he thought I didn't know what I was choosing. The Lord changed the "major's" mind and he gave us a letter saying we were free to go out. He also released Charles Mann from prison.

SATURDAY, 21st. Steven Scholten fretful and had temperature in the evening. By 10 p.m. he was twitching and delirious, temperature 103.4 F. We all prayed for him. The "major" visited us and then supplied the guards with guns.

SUNDAY, 22ND. I got up at 2 a.m. to Sandy, who was crying, but could not comfort her. The doctor was released from prison.

MONDAY, 23RD. Hardly any sleep. Someone tried to get in about 2 a.m. but I didn't answer the door. The guard knew we were in difficulties and at 4 o'clock he did his inspection and inquired if any of the children were dead. The Simbas became very excited and quarrelsome and we heard rumours of a surrender in Stanleyville. About 4 p.m. we heard shouting in the near vicinity and we were hidden in a store room. After fifteen minutes a party of white men appeared on the verandah and suddenly, oh so suddenly, we found ourselves free. The mercenaries had arrived!

We talked and talked and I went to have a bath. That night the doctor asked me to go with him to help to deliver a baby. I set off with a song of rejoicing in my heart — "Sing unto the Lord with thanksgiving, sing praise upon the harp unto our God" (Psalm 147, v. 7).

TUESDAY, 24TH. We went to see Bill's grave. There was no identifying memorial, just a mound of earth.

On Thursday, 26th November, the Aketi group were flown to Bumba and then on to Leopoldville where they met Al Larson and the other U.F.M. missionaries who had been liberated earlier. Before leaving, the party was approached by a group of mercenaries. Several hung awkwardly in the background while their spokesman approached the young widow shepherding her five small children and tried to find words to say. But words were impossible to one whose ministry it was to minister to the spiritual needs of others. He simply extended his hand, revealing a crumpled pile of bank notes. "Ma'am," he said, "We've had a whip round", and then they went back to the war.

CHAPTER NINE

OPERATION RESCUE

ALTHOUGH DARKNESS had fallen on that fateful day of November 24th, Leopoldville Airport was still alive with activity. Scores of officials, soldiers, doctors, newspaper reporters, as well as thousands of civilians awaiting news of their friends or relatives, hung around the busy airport. Ambulances flashed on and off the runways with their cargoes of pain. All day plane loads of hostages had been flown from Stanleyville and, as the hands of the clock pointed to 9 p.m., yet another plane containing 115 white hostages was due to land in a C.130 box-type aircraft. The engine roared as the plane skimmed the tops of the buildings while the clappers looked aghast. The landing wheels had failed to descend. The plane nosed up again, encircled the airport and came in for a second try. Again the landing gear failed. With the fourth approach the wheels came down and 115 thankful hostages set their feet on the ground, a thousand miles from the scene where they had been within seconds of death.

The U.F.M. family gathered at the Union Mission House and exchanged their experiences. Al Larson reported the horror of their rude awakening and forced march down the street, the last speech of "colonel" Opepe and his flight to safety. David and Sonia Grant told of their strange experiences living amidst the ritual of Catholic nuns and priests. Mr. and Mrs. Jenkinson, Miss Mary Rutt and Mr. and Mrs. V. Gscheidle told of the sale of 1,000 Testaments in the L.E.C.O. Headquarters during the occupation. Then they told each other what they had seen and heard over the last weeks. In addition to the whites who had suffered brutality and death, many hundreds of Congolese had been slain. In spite of the

torrential tropical rain the memorial steps at the foot of the
Patrice Lumumba monument were stained red. All those
who had learned how to read and write or had received
education abroad, or had been associated with western
capitalism in any way whatsoever were the targets of the
rebels. Some had been tortured to death, some had been
slain with the long Congolese knife known as a machette,
and frequently the rebels had eaten the hearts of their victims.

Then came the Carlson story. Dr. Paul Carlson did not
arrive in Stanleyville until October 23rd although he had
been arrested in Yakoma 310 miles to the north a month
earlier. He was a marked prisoner and "President" Gbenye
spoke mysteriously about a certain U.S. major who was spying
for the imperialists. It was some days before Carlson realised
that they were referring to him. On one occasion Carlson
and several others imprisoned with him were taken to the
Lumumba monument and were shown bullets and machettes
which the rebels said they were going to use to kill them.
The execution did not take place and the hostages were
driven to Gbenye's residence. There "President" Gbenye
announced that Dr. Carlson's execution had been postponed
owing to an appeal by Kenya's Prime Minister, Jomo
Kenyatta. The hostages imprisoned with Carlson were not
missionaries and Carlson wisely had never talked about
his faith, but on their return from this incident he suddenly
said, "Wait a minute. Let's pray", and everyone did. After
that, several times Carlson was told that the hour of his
execution had been fixed, but on each occasion it was postponed. He was later transferred to the Victoria Hotel and
was shot while attempting to escape in Avenue Sergeant
Kitele. Al had seen Carlson's body with a label tied around
his neck lying at the side of the road awaiting burial. His
body was flown to a little cemetery at Karawa, a mission
station where he had worked as a missionary doctor and
had become loved by the Congolese. As the coffin was unloaded from the plane a man called out, "He saved my life",
and many Africans crowded alongside to catch a glimpse

of the one who had served them so faithfully. Even in prison he had treated the wounds of over fifty rebel soldiers in one day.

Then came another testimony from Al Larson. After he had been arrested he was ordered on to a truck and was told that they were going to Banalia as there were too many hostages in Stanleyville. After only one and a half miles outside Stanleyville the tarmac road disappears and as the badly maintained vehicle bumped along the rough clay roadway it came to a halt. The rebels were furious. The hostages were allowed to descend from their cramped quarters and the driver asked if any of them knew how to repair a lorry. At first no one volunteered, but when the rebels became abusive one Belgian stepped forward and said he could put right the fault. He took off his coat, mended the fault, but successfully jammed the gasoline, rendering the vehicle quite useless. The hostages were marched back into Stanley-ville.

Many Roman Catholic stations had fared far worse than their Protestant counterparts. Groups of nuns had been molested, stripped and beaten. A Mother Superior of a mission hospital at Bondamba, 300 miles north-west of Stanleyville, owned a tiny transistor radio. Simbas in leopard skins appeared in mid-September and accused her of sending messages to the Americans. They returned a few weeks later, killed the cows of the mission, and stole chickens and rice. On their next visit they abducted several schoolgirls and spent the night in sniffing dope made from locally grown hemp. Finally, they arrested the Mother Superior, forced her to strip and locked her in a room with sixteen other nuns and twenty-three priests. Stories of atrocities multiplied. A bank manager was horribly mutilated for refusing to open the vaults of his bank. A Government official was taken outside the city, killed, and then buried half in the ground and half out, leaving the upper part of his body exposed. Streets were often littered with dead, and sometimes they remained unburied for several days.

At one place a row of Congolese prisoners were made to lie on the ground and then at an order from the rebel lieutenant the soldiers jumped on them until they were dead. It seemed that the rebel leaders were intoxicated by blood. They ordered their Simbas to wear amulets and persuaded them that they were invulnerable. During attacks they would yell "Mai-Mulele" or "Mai-Olenga", magic formulae which they believed would change their enemies' bullets into drops of water.

On top of the killings came stories of witchcraft, drug addiction and unbelievable sorceries. The witch doctor and the sorceress played an important part in the command of the rebels. At Kindu it was common to see General Nicolas Olenga, Commander in Chief of the rebel forces, confer with a well-known sorceress, Mama Onoma, and then make use of her prophecies to hold his army spell-bound.

A paratroop drop on Paulis on Thursday, November 26th, brought news of yet another massacre. At least seventeen white people were killed, one of whom was Mr. J. Tucker of the Assemblies of God Mission. It was reported that he was blinded with a broken bottle after which his arms were tied behind his back and then his wrists were tied to his ankles and he was bent in a backward arch, after which he was beaten for forty-five minutes and then thrown into the river. The heart of man is wicked and so are his deeds and all the brutality and bestiality that can be imprisoned within a man's soul was unleashed. However, this further paratroop drop was the means of rescuing many hostages although one paratrooper was killed and five wounded in the operation. A few days later the Baptist Missionary Society station at Yakusu was liberated and all the missionaries were saved. One of the nurses, Miss June Moors, was being dragged by a Simba to a canoe at the river bank. Her companion, nurse Doreen West, gallantly ran to her rescue. She got her free, but in doing so she was badly bruised about the face, and her arm was slashed with a machette. The nurses were able to get

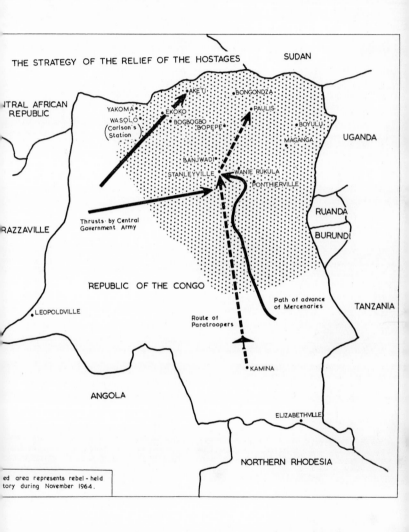

THE STRATEGY OF THE RELIEF OF THE HOSTAGES

SUDAN

CENTRAL AFRICAN REPUBLIC

AKETI • BONGONDZA

YAKOMA • PAULIS

EKOKO • BOGBOGBO

WASOLO BOPEPE BOYULU

(Carlson's Station) MAGANGA UGANDA

BANJWADI

STANLEYVILLE • WANIE RUKULA

PONTHIERVILLE

RUANDA

BURUNDI

Thrusts by Central Government Army

BRAZZAVILLE

REPUBLIC OF THE CONGO

TANZANIA

Path of advance of Mercenaries

LEOPOLDVILLE

Route of Paratroopers

• KAMINA

ANGOLA

ELIZABETHVILLE •

NORTHERN RHODESIA

...ed area represents rebel-held
...tory during November 1964.

Miss Erskine, Mrs. Southard and the McAllisters arriving at the airfield.

The first party arrived home on November 30th. They were Rev. and Mrs. H. Jenkins and Miss Mina Erskine.

The second party arrived home on the 1st December, and consisted of Mr. and Mrs. R. McAllister and Family, Rev. and Mrs. M. Southard and Larry (above) and Miss Betty O'Neill.

The Rev. J. Hector McMillan.

The Rev. and Mrs. H. Jenkinson and their bookmobile, which often carried Scriptures in 12 languages.

Rescued ! The mercenaries reach the house in which the Aketi group was under arrest.

The progressive church at Banalia which was pastored by a national.

The maternity hospital at Ekoko where Miss Hiles and Miss O'Neill were working. Expectant mothers were left in the wards when the missionaries were arrested.

The maternity hospital at Boyulu.

A sick child is treated by the witchdoctor,
who ties charms onto her hair to
drive out evil spirits.

A Sunday School class held in the open a
at Ekoko by a national evangelist
using flannelgraph.

The Banjwadi Bible Institute—one of the
five Seminaries in Congo which had
attained Theological College status.

The first pygmy converts are baptised
Pastors Asani and Jenkinson. The pygm
are despised by their fellow countrym
and tend to become neglected by
missionari

back to the hospital where they hid until they considered it safe to make their way to the house of Dr. Taylor who was able to stitch up the wound in semi-darkness and without an anaesthetic. When Mike Hoare's mercenaries arrived the following day, their ordeal was over.

After the exchange of stories and experiences there was a time of fellowship. The Word of God had become very precious during the days of captivity and prayer had seemed real. Now they had been liberated and were free to witness again. The Rev. Ralph Odman, General Secretary of the U.F.M. in the U.S.A., together with Mr. Homer Dowdy, a journalist and writer, went out to the missionaries and together they discussed immediate plans. It was agreed that all who had been freed should return to their homeland for a period of rest owing to the immense strain to which they had been subjected, particularly as it would be impossible to reach the bush stations for a considerable while. Thus, Mr. and Mrs. Jenkinson, Mr. and Mrs. Gscheidle and Miss Mina Erskine left first, arriving home on the 30th November, 1964. They were followed by Mr. and Mrs. Carper and Marilyn, Mrs. McMillan and her six children, the Misses Walker and Bjerkseth and Hiles, Mr. and Mrs. Grant, Mrs. Scholten and her children, Mr. and Mrs. Mann and two children, who went direct to the United States, and Mr. and Mrs. McAllister and their family, Rev. and Mrs. Southard and Larry, and Miss Betty O'Neill, who arrived home on 1st December, 1964. Only one thing marred the rejoicing of liberation. They left twenty-one fellow workers and children still in the hands of the Simbas.

CHAPTER TEN

ON THE EDGE OF THE RIPPLE

UNFORTUNATELY MR. TSHOMBE was not popular in many countries right from the beginning, probably due to his close association with the West. He flew to Egypt to attend a conference of African Prime Ministers but was refused admittance. Later he decided to visit Italy, West Germany and Belgium on an economic expedition. In July he had conferences with the Italian Minister for External Trade, in Rome he was received by Pope Paul VI, and in West Germany he visited Munich, Bonn and Dusseldorf, where he had talks with industrialists and financiers and, finally, he went to Belgium at the invitation of the Foreign Minister, Mr. Paul-Henri Spaak, but wherever he went he needed a strong guard and he was faced with constant demonstrations against him.

The effects of the parachute drops on Stanleyville and Paulis vibrated throughout the world. There was a violent demonstration in Moscow where more than one thousand African and Asian students demonstrated outside the British, American, Belgian and Congolese Embassies. For over three hours they yelled slogans and hurled sticks and police had to force demonstrators off the railings outside the American Embassy. The Congolese Ambassador's study was raided and many of his official papers and files were thrown into the street. Seven hundred African and Yugoslav students made a similar demonstration in Belgrade denouncing the Belgian/American aggression in the Congo and in several other world capitals there were identical demonstrations of feeling. Moreover, Prime Minister Tshombe found it necessary to lodge a complaint to Algeria, Egypt and Sudan for assisting the rebel forces in Congo against the legal Government of the land. On December 9th he wrote the following letter to His Majesty Emperor Haile Selassie of Ethiopia:

"Your Majesty,

Events affecting the sovereignty and independence of the democratic republic of the Congo have recently occurred. If allowed to continue, they will endanger peace and stability, not only in the Congo, but in the whole of Africa.

Disregarding the provisions of the U.N.O. Charter and the resolution of the Security Council of July 20th, 1960 (S/4405) whereby every state should abstain from any action tantamount to preventing the restoration of public order and the exercise of its authority by the Congolese Government, and also from any action likely to destroy the territorial integrity and political independence of the Congo Republic, some countries have been helping rebel groups in the eastern area of the Congo.

In this respect, the position of the Algerian Government is particularly disturbing since not only has the Algerian President publicly announced that his country is helping the rebels in supplying them with men and weapons, but observers have also reported the presence in the Sudan, near the Congolese frontier, of aircraft with registration numbers from Algeria. The Sudanese Government has moreover admitted that some transports to the rebels had been carried out without the agreement of the legal Government of the Congo. Other occurrences tend to prove that the Governments of the U.A.R. and Ghana are closely linked with the assistance to the rebels.

On top of the well-known political support of Communist China to the rebels my Government has discovered in the Congo some arms and ammunition made in China.

Furthermore, we are concerned by some press reports that the Soviet Union would be agreeable to supply arms to the Congolese rebels and to help finance the cost of their air transport which is done by the U.A.R. and Algeria.

Such violations of the sovereignty of a country, member of the U.N.O., in defiance of all principles of international law and of

the U.N.O. Charter, constitute an inadmissible intervention in
my country's internal affairs and should cease forthwith.

In consequence, I request your Majesty, Mr. Secretary-General,
Mr. President to convene urgently the Security Council to examine
the problem of this foreign interference with the internal affairs
of the Congo, an interference which, if allowed to go on, will
constitute a serious threat to peace in Africa.

I am also sending the same message to the Secretary-General of
the Organisation for African Unity with the request to circulate it
to all country members of this organisation for their information.

I assure you, Your Majesty, of my very high consideration.

MOISE TSHOMBE."

The Belgian Minister of Foreign Affairs was called by the
Security Council to make a statement on December 11th,
which he did. He stated, "I have heard seven or eight indict-
ments, but I can assure you that I have not come here to
stand in the dock as the accused, to plead attenuating or
extenuating circumstances before a court.   I come here
strengthened by my rights and by my conscience, sure of
being supported by the immense majority of the public opinion
of my country and, I also believe, encouraged and sustained
by the stated or tacit approval of many Governments all
over the world . . . The truth of the matter is that in Stanleyville the situation became progressively worse and progressively
more dangerous.   Belgians and Americans were arrested,
they were threatened, they were harrassed, they were humiliated, and finally they were imprisoned.   On 30th October
the following message was intercepted — 'We can no longer
guarantee the lives of Belgian and American nationals'.   On
2nd November, in radio messages addressed to Messrs.
Nkrumah, Ben Bella, Nasser, and Sekou Toure, Gbenye
threatened to carry out a scorched-earth policy.   He said:
'The popular army of liberation has always protected foreigners
but it will do so no longer with respect to nationals of certain
countries, the Governments of which are assisting the
imperialist Moise Tshombe. Because of the bombings —'

"And, gentlemen, I give you formal assurance that there never was a single bombing of Stanleyville before 24th November — "

'Because of the bombings all Americans and Belgians in the liberated areas are to be considered as prisoners of war . . . '

"What were we to do? 'Nothing', certain people said. 'Take the risk of allowing them to be murdered, or else take the risk' — I knew that there was a risk and I know it still better today — yes, 'take the risk of trying to rescue them'. We waited until the last possible moment before taking our decision. It is true that we went from Belgium to Ascension Island where the British had offered us hospitality. We did not want to go to the Congo immediately because, up to the very last moment, you may or may not believe me when I say this, but I am sure that the great majority of people will believe me, we hoped that we would not have to act . . . We landed in Stanleyville on the 24th. On the 27th everyone was back in Kamina and on the 29th there was not a single Belgian soldier of the paratroopers who had been sent to Stanleyville or Paulis on Congolese soil, the rescue operation was finished."

Mr. Spaak went on to outline his country's policy toward Congo when he again referred to the parachute drop —

"There is no interference in the internal affairs of a country when the legal Government of that country is given the assistance that that Government has requested. There is interference in the internal affairs of a country when, against the legal Government, rebellion or revolution is upheld. If anyone has another explanation or definition of non-interference to submit, I should like to hear it for I believe that, for the health of the United Nations, we ought to know once and for all what non-interference actually means".

Great Britain was also active at this time because there were still eighteen U.F.M. missionaries not accounted for: the group at Banalia, the party at Bafwensende and Rev. and Mrs. George Kerrigan who were last heard of at Bunia.

Mr. Anthony Fell, M.P. for Yarmouth, tried to get an emergency debate in the House of Commons and more than fifty M.P.s signed a motion calling for immediate rescue steps. The Foreign Minister was asked to take immediate action, which he promised to do, although subsequently said that a British parachute drop was unthinkable. *The parachute drops in Congo were like a brick thrown in a pond which makes ripples over the surface to the furthermost edges, so this one action reverberated throughout the world and on the edges of the ripples were the three home base offices, situated at 9, Gunnersbury Avenue, London, W.5., Bala-Cynwyd, Philadelphia, U.S.A., and Melbourne, Australia.* In London the Secretaries' office was turned into an information bureau. The telephone rang constantly throughout the day and often well into the night. Distressed relatives, prayer partners, team supporters, newspaper writers, journalists and ministers were all wanting news from Congo. A large map of Congo was pinned to the wall, spattered by flags indicating the positions of rebel-held towns and the movement of the National Army troops and pinpointing the towns where it was believed our missionaries were trapped. Every news bulletin was received and carefully recorded and so for four months the constant stream of calls and queries went on. Prayer meetings commenced all over the country, in Europe, Australia, and in U.S.A. for those still lost in Congo.

In the late evening of the 27th August 1964 the *Daily Express* telephoned saying that Miss J. Erskine was "missing" and asked Headquarters to supply details. Unfortunately, the London Office had received no news and neither had the Foreign Office any information. Meanwhile paragraphs appeared in several papers reporting the tragic occurrence and causing much distress to her relatives.

It transpired that Mr. Harms, who was in Uganda, had sent in a list of missionaries and their last known whereabouts, but unfortunately omitted Miss Erskine. Thus a *Daily Express* reporter, on comparing the list supplied by Mr. Harms and the list of names of those known to be in Congo given by London, reported one as missing. In actual fact she was never out of the company of the others at Kilometre 8! The Rev. Marshall Southard, who was in Leopoldville at the outbreak of the crisis, acted as liaison officer though unfortunately he did not have a typewriter at first and thus had to write hundreds of letters in longhand, often making copies of letters from Africans to send both to the United Kingdom and the United States of America. The information that he was able to supply and advice he gave proved invaluable as he was the only connecting link between the London and U.S.A. headquarters and the field. In fact, he was kept so busy collecting information and forwarding it that sometimes he did not have time to go to bed. During this period negotiations were carried on with the Red Cross International to try to secure the release of the remaining missionaries and also careful plans were made so that there was money available to bring them home and also to provide accommodation.

Whilst in Leopoldville, Mr. Larson and Mr. Odman made a continual round of the embassies urging them to send a party to relieve Banalia, Bafwensende and Bunia, and those on the edge of the ripple worked and prayed to secure the release of the remainder of God's servants.

CHAPTER ELEVEN

STRANGE NEIGHBOURS

THE REV. GEORGE KERRIGAN sailed to Congo in May 1922, while Mrs. Dora Kerrigan sailed in September 1926. They met and married on the field in 1928. The Kerrigans are born pioneers and have always worked where the going was rough and the need was great. While stationed at Boyulu in 1932 Mr. Kerrigan visited Maganga and immediately realised that here was a village area completely unevangelized and one which would be an ideal evangelistic centre. They began to pray for the people of Maganga and shortly after the way opened for them to move in and commence building. Little did they realise that more than 20 years of their lives were to be spent on this station, both preaching, building and directing the work from stage to stage. During those twenty years they saw many huge forest giants hewn down and the ground levelled and then new buildings rising in which children would receive both an education and an introduction to the Saviour, and a dispensary where their wounds could be treated and where they would hear of the remedy for sin.

Once Maganga was well established they moved to another completely untouched area called Wanie Rukula. Commencing in 1954 they worked in this neglected area occupied by backward and difficult people, but believing that no task was too difficult for God, they preached faithfully, and over the course of ten years saw more than 200 converts, the majority of whom were baptised by Mr. Kerrigan. In 1962 the believers subscribed towards the building of their own church which was well designed and constructed from cement blocks. Mr. Volker Gscheidle helped considerably with the building programme. During these ten years the Kerrigans visited Ponthierville on the extreme southern edge of the U.F.M. allocated area and eventually Mr. and Mrs. R. McAllister established themselves in this town to present the claims of Christ.

It so happened that Wanie Rukula was one of the first towns to fall to the rebels but Mr. and Mrs. Kerrigan were on holiday in Uganda. Thinking the rising was but a local skirmish they made their way back into Congo and tried to get to Boyulu where there was a large party of U.F.M. missionaries, but owing to road blocks they only got as far as Bunia. This town is in the Africa Inland Mission allocated area but they found that all the missionaries had already withdrawn so they occupied the abandoned field secretary's house. In one sense they were quite well off. This area of Congo is healthy, wide open country surrounded by hills, and blessed with moderate sunshine and frequent breezes. Many missionaries go to Bunia for a vacation and all went well with the Kerrigans until a party of Simbas arrived and lodged in the empty house next door! Then they began their usual routine of destroying the previous civilisation and rebuilding their own. They went from house to house and office to office. All records relating to finance, pensions, taxes, etc. were thrown out of the windows and some were burned. Houses were looted and everything of value was carried off. Bunia was the home of a faithful Congolese pastor named Zebedayo. When Simbas searched his house they found a photograph of President Kasavubu and this was sufficient evidence to associate him with the National Government. While his house was systematically pillaged his hands were tied behind his back and then his feet tied together. He was knocked to the floor and a rope was passed from hands to feet and drawn tight. The only movement that he could make was rolling from side to side and raising his head. He was ordered to "confess" that he had been transmitting to the Americans, but as he did not own a transmitter obviously he could not confess. So he protested his innocence. The Simbas then brought a pail of water and told him to drink, pushing his head into it. By the time they let him withdraw his head he was gasping for breath. He still said he was innocent. The "colonel" drew his bayonet and, prodding the pastor in his back, told him he had fifteen minutes to confess or he would be killed. The "colonel" timed the fifteen minutes on his wrist watch but still the faithful pastor refused to let an untruth pass from his lips. By the intervention of God, his life was spared and he was sent to a military camp. A Christian woman named Cecilia, who had joined the Simba ranks and knew the "colonel", sought his release and although this was promised it was not carried out. That weekend the "colonel" organised a rally of youth intending to enlist many into the rebel movement. They marched through the streets singing at the tops of their voices, "The flesh of Mr. Tshombe is very sweet. We will eat it with our cooked rice". Then the "colonel" decided to dispose of some of his prisoners. He sent a lorry to the prison and it was loaded with those who had displeased the new *regime*. At first the lorry would not start so the prisoners had to push it. Then they were made to run a couple of miles. When they reached the "colonel" he asked each man why he was in prison. He put nine on one side and sent the others back to prison, including Pastor Zebedayo. The nine singled out were then lined up and shot. Again the Christian woman went to see the "colonel" and asked him why the pastor was not set free if he was innocent. Much prayer was made for him and that weekend the pastor was released.

A Roman Catholic priest in Bunia was accused of telling his school children that great trouble was coming to Congo and the complete staff of the school were arrested. While they were away the rebels entered the station and took all provisions and stores for feeding the children as well as all the money that they could find. All round about them were murders, torturings and robbery, leaving ugly scars across the town which would take a long time to heal. Being quite near the border it was sometimes possible for the Kerrigans to write home and in a letter to the General Secretary dated 22nd November they wrote: " 'Roll all your burdens on the Lord'. It is what we are doing but they come back again so it keeps us continually praying. We know the Lord will undertake and we pray that He will spare all hostages. We still keep well, though we have practically no medicines for fever, but rich fellowship each day with visitors from the church." Surprisingly enough, the Kerrigans got on very well with their strange neighbours, the Simbas. Mrs. Kerrigan carried on pleasant conversations across the fence in the garden though the Simbas were disappointed when she told them that they did not have any whiskey. One day they accepted New Testaments from her and they made no attempt to prevent them visiting the town and giving out tracts or visiting the homes of Congolese. On one occasion they were wakened about 2 o'clock in the morning by a persistent banging on the door. They both got up.

"Open the door, open the door," repeated the "commander".

"We never open the door at night time to strangers," replied the Kerrigans, "Please come back in the morning and we will see to your needs."

"But I am the commander and I want somewhere to stay the night."

"The best hours of the night have already gone, and there is nowhere you can sleep here for we are lodging in this house. Try next door."

"Open the door, open the door. I want to come in."

"We cannot open the door. We are not dressed and we do not see visitors at nighttime. Come back in the morning."

After that they remained silent and although the banging and shouting persisted for some time the unwelcome visitors eventually went away. The Kerrigans were also fortunate in being able to retain the radio set so they heard regular broadcasts from London and knew that a column of mercenaries were on their way to Bunia to relieve them. Three weeks later than expected, the mercenaries arrived. As a crocodile of vehicles drove into the town their guns spat fire from each side, spraying the houses and any Africans who happened to be in sight. The Kerrigans lay on the floor in the basement. This was a wise precaution for they found more than ten bullets had plastered the wall and had broken the bedroom window. After the vehicles had driven around the town for a couple of hours raking everywhere with gunfire, they searched the houses and the Kerrigans were brought through to safety. They flew to Leopoldville and then on to London, arriving on 10th December, 1964. Thus ended more than forty years of pioneer work in Congo. They returned to the homeland having truly earned a place in the roll of heroes of faith, for they faced similar circumstances to the Victors listed in Hebrews 11.

"Who through faith subdued kingdoms, wrought righteousness, obtained promises, stopped the mouths of lions, quenched the violence of fire, escaped the edge of the sword, out of weakness were made strong, waxed valiant in fight, turned to flight the armies of the aliens . . . " (Hebrews 11, vs. 33, 34).

CHAPTER TWELVE

SAVED TO SERVE

SINCE THE EARLY DAYS of the Church God has called out men and women to forward His purposes and has laid His hand on them, frequently from their earliest days and prepared them for His service. This was certainly the case with the majority of those who eventually found that their paths crossed at Banalia.

Audrey Mary Gibson was born in May 1932 in Lincoln and grew to be a lovely, happy child. Almost as soon as she could walk she enjoyed playing with her dolls and always wanted to be a nurse. Her favourite pastime was to pretend that her dolls were sick and injured and she would tend them with "medicines" and bandage them. She loved her Sunday school and enjoyed taking part in various plays at the church as well as partaking in Brownie and Girl Guide activities. She constantly invited her friends to join her Pack and often walked miles to meet them and take them to meetings. Her desire to nurse never wavered throughout her childhood or school days and during those early years she moved towards thinking in the terms of a "missionary nurse". When she was only six years old her father, who was a decorator and painter in Lincoln, died. The loss of the bread-winner was a tremendous blow to the household but Mrs. Gibson had a real faith in God and committed her way to Him, asking that she might faithfully provide for, and guide, her two daughters aged six and seven and a half. She took in lodgers in order to keep the girls at the South Park High School in Lincoln until they passed their General Certificates of Education. This examination Audrey obtained at the age of sixteen, and was still determined to be a missionary nurse. Her mother stood firmly behind her and longed to see her daughter doing the job for which she felt called and took her to see the matron at Branston Hall Sanatorium for advice. The matron advised that she should commence her tuberculosis training immediately and then go on to a general hospital for the remainder. This she did and joined the staff of Mildmay Mission Hospital, London, in order to study for her S.R.N. She frequently visited her mother and loved her home church, which was the Thomas Cooper Memorial Church, Lincoln. It was here that she had been instructed in the Word of God from her earliest days, where she heard the needs of the mission field and where she was converted and baptised. As her training progressed her regular letters to her mother included some information about a doctor friend and a weekend was arranged when he should be introduced to the family. It was not without heart-searching and embarrassment that Audrey brought her friend home and as the door opened Mrs. Gibson caught first sight of a smart young man dressed in a blue-grey suit with his university scarf around his neck.

"Mother," began Audrey, "this is Ian Sharpe. He is our casualty officer and he is going to be a missionary."

After that introduction Ian became a frequent visitor to the Gibson household and at the end of 1954 Audrey proudly displayed her engagement ring with a deep blue sapphire stone in the centre and a diamond on either side. They were married on 2nd July, 1955.

Ian Maurice Sharpe also came from a Christian family and for many years his father served as a lay pastor of a church. Ian was educated at Brockley County Grammar School and his brilliant intellect soon won him the position of head boy. The headmaster realising his capabilities, recommended that he should be trained for a senior Civil Service position, but Ian had other ideas.

At the age of fourteen he had been converted through the faithful ministry of his Sunday school teacher and when he was eighteen felt a call to become a medical missionary.

Surprisingly enough, he had felt faint at the sight of blood up to the age of seven, but God prepared him for the task that lay ahead and gave him "steel" nerves and "cast-iron" confidence. While his parents and headmaster were still discussing his future he made his own application to Guy's Hospital and commenced to study medicine. In steady succession he passed the M.B., B.S. (Lond.), L.R.C.P., M.R.C.S., D.T.M., and the first part of the F.R.C.S. He was one of fourteen successful candidates out of a total entry of seventy-two in the latter examination. On completion of training he was called up for National Service and he became a captain in the R.A.M.C., serving in Jamaica, British Honduras and Bermuda. While in Jamaica he was invited by the Governor to attend the reception in 1953 for the visit of Her Majesty the Queen, and when in Bermuda he was medical officer on call during the time of the conference between Messrs. Churchill, Stalin and Truman. He had the unusual experience of being baptised by his own father in April 1945 at Allerford Road Baptist Church, Catford, S.E.6, and the baptismal text was John 15, v. 16: "Ye have not chosen Me, but I have chosen you".

Ian and Audrey Sharpe sailed to Congo in 1956 and were first stationed at Ekoko and subsequently at Bongondza. Ian was a gifted surgeon and his deftness of touch and neatness in the operating theatre made him not only a master of his profession but endeared him to the Congolese. As a musician he was in the ranks of the foremost non-professionals and he was a powerful preacher and evangelist. In spite of these qualities it would have been hard to find a more humble follower of the Lord Jesus Christ. Ian and Audrey were a perfect team, Ian doing the operating, Audrey acting as his anaesthetist or theatre assistant. Their names will always be associated with the Bongondza hospital.

This hospital was developed by Dr. Norman Streight from the U.S.A. He started to rebuild it, but owing to the evacuation in 1960 it was not completed. Dr. Sharpe arrived at Bongondza on 15th July 1961 and immediately set about

renovating the building. A generous gift of an electric
generator from a friend in Ireland enabled the hospital to
have electricity installed for the first time. There were two
wards, one for men and one for women containing twenty
beds each and in addition six houses in which the tubercular
patients lived. The remainder of the hospital consisted of a
dispensary, a consulting room for out-patients, a laboratory
and pharmacy, a maternity unit, seven houses and a workshop.
Ian had a tremendous capacity for work. At 6.30 a.m. he
supervised a morning clinic for children (every other week)
after which he went home for breakfast. At 8 o'clock there
was a service in the hospital, usually conducted by a Congolese evangelist and at 8.30 he commenced his round of the
wards, finishing up in the consulting room to see any difficult
cases. Meanwhile the operating theatre would have been
prepared by Audrey and from 9.30 - 12 they would operate
(two or three times weekly). From 12 - 2 there was a rest
period but which included lunch and a time with the children.
The afternoon was spent in doing paper work, filling in
Government forms, attending specialist clinics, checking
medicine and supplies and sterilizing the theatre and equipment. At 5 o'clock they went home for tea and spent a while
with their children before family prayers and bed. Every
night in their home from 7 - 7.30 there was a prayer meeting
for all missionaries, after which Ian would go back to the
hospital to check serious cases and those upon whom he had
operated that day. Then came a time of study, prayer and
preparation of his messages for his evangelistic work. At
10 o'clock they would go to bed, Audrey would turn over
to sleep but Ian would study for another two hours endeavouring to keep up with the march of medical science. In addition
to his plan to sit his final F.R.C.S. examination during his
next furlough which he considered essential, he took two
correspondence courses with the London Bible College. On
one occasion he read in a medical journal of a method to
perform a caesarian section in a case of emergency or under
primitive conditions, known as the symphysi-otomy, which

Rev. and Mrs. G. Kerrigan

Dr. and Mrs. Ian Sharpe
Jillian, Alison and Andrew

Miss Mary Baker.

Mr. and Mrs. Denny Parry and family.

Miss Robina Gray.

The ferry landing at Banalia—the scene of the killing of Dr. and Mrs. Sharpe and family, Mr. and Mrs. Parry and their two youngest children, Miss Ruby Gray and Miss Mary Baker.

was dividing a bone to allow birth using only a local anaesthetic. Several days later Miss Ruby Gray called him to an
emergency case requiring a caesarian section but the operating
theatre was being repaired. It was impossible to sterilise it
in time but he remembered the diagrams and instruction
of his magazine. Although he had never seen the operation
done he performed it successfully and saved the lives of both
mother and baby.

After the rebel takeover he heard the order given by the
rebel chief for all white people to report to the nearest large
town and he broadcast over the inter-station radio that he
was planning to go to Banalia on the following day with
Audrey and their three children, Jillian Lynn, aged eight;
Alison Joy, aged seven, and Andrew, aged four. The pastor,
Masini Phillipe and his son, Mbongo Samuel, refused to
let him go alone. Only a short while before the doctor had
saved Masini's life when the Simbas arrested him with the
intention of shooting him because he had previously supported
an opposing political party. Thus the family packed their
bags and made their way to Banalia in accordance with the
orders of the prevailing ruling body.

*   *   *

Dennis Edward Parry was the youngest of a family of six
and as his father was left a widower his boyhood was not
particularly happy. He attended Holmesdale Road Baptist
Church, South Norwood, and was very keen on the Boys'
Brigade. In 1936 he transferred to the Portland Road Mission,
South Norwood, to assist in the newly formed B.B. company
there, where he attained the rank of Staff Sergeant. Converted at the age of 20, he subsequently attended the Keswick
Convention in 1937 and responded to the challenge at the
missionary meeting. War had already broken out when he
was applying to several colleges and he felt very definitely
that the call of God must be put before the call to National
Service. Several colleges refused his application on this

ground and when he appeared before the tribunal to register as a conscientious objector this, too, was rejected. He still refused to serve in the Armed Forces knowing that God wanted him in Congo as soon as possible and was sentenced to imprisonment. He continued to witness even though deprived of liberty and on his release was accepted by a college and later by U.F.M. He sailed for Congo in 1948 and, having a passion for souls, loved the work of village evangelism. However, being a general handyman he also undertook the maintenance of Mission property and assisted in erecting new buildings.

Nora Magee Parry spent her early years working with the Christian Endeavour and in the open air. She received her missionary call when reading a missionary article in the U.F.M. magazine written by the Rev. George Kerrigan. He recounted how the Congolese had built homes ready for missionaries to go and minister to them but there were no missionaries available to accept their open invitation. Thus, Nora dedicated her life to Christ and applied to the Mayday Hospital, Croydon, to study nursing. Overcoming her slender education she trained first as a nurse and then attended the Mount Hermon Missionary Training College. Although she had known Dennis during childhood there was no engagement nor understanding between them when they sailed for the field. They married while on the field and three of their four children were born in Congo. In the latter years Nora suffered much with her health. At one time the ulcers on her legs were so bad that she could not walk and she had to be carried to the dispensary on a chair. But still she pressed on, refusing to rest, both tending the sick and making known the name of Christ. During the last few months they settled at a bush station known as Bodela at the invitation of local believers, as they had not previously had a resident missionary. It was from Bodela that Mr. and Mrs. Parry, together with their two younger children, Andrew John, aged 11, and Grace Edith, aged 9, were taken to Banalia during the rising. Their two elder children, Hazel Charlotte, aged fourteen, and

Stephen Keith, aged thirteen, remained at home after the last furlough of their parents in order to complete their education. Neither Dennis nor Nora Parry ever found their names in the headlines, nor was there anything of a spectacular nature to highlight their missionary career, but their faithful and persistent witness brought a harvest of souls. They worked on new buildings — kept open the doors of the dispensary — helped in village evangelism and assisted a multitude of "projects". One such was the adult school which they were asked to supervise by the Field Conference in 1955. Just after the school opened Nora Parry wrote to headquarters:

"In an effort to help establish the Christians in the faith, an afternoon school has been started this week. The session is to last for six months. During that time those who cannot read will be taught (if it is at all possible!) so that all can have the privilege of reading the Bible for themselves. Doctrine and Personal Evangelism are on the curriculum as well as the three R's and Hygiene and First Aid, and we have fourteen men and women studying for the first six months. They have an hour's teaching from 6.30 a.m. to 7.30 a.m. and from 8 till 12 they do manual work about the station. Then from 2 to 4.30 they are in school. They will be paid a small wage for this work they do. Dennis has been given charge of this school and this is the first week: what with that and dispensary work and a family we find our time fully occupied. Already folks are handing in their names for the next session. It will certainly meet a real need for these folk do need grounding in the faith and to be taught to seek out the lost and try to lead them to the Saviour. Their attitude so often is 'I am alright — that is sufficient'. Please join with us in prayer for this project."

Thus they made their lives count for the Lord's work in Congo.

*   *   *

Miss Mary Elizabeth Baker was born at Richmond, Virginia, U.S.A., and trained for the mission field at the Moody Bible Institute, Chicago. She was a precious worker of the Mission, a dear friend to many of the missionaries, and beloved by the Congolese. All through the Congo crisis of Independence she lived right among the people, sharing their joys and sorrows, hopes and fears. To live in her little house which had been built by the Congolese for her was a revelation of the esteem in which she was held. At any time in the day, anyone needing help, anyone in sorrow, any of the large group of women of the community could drop in. Soon they were seated, maybe having a cup of coffee or a drink of water, and getting refreshment for body and soul. Mary loved them all, and they loved her — one could see it in their shining faces. The last church meetings held at Bopepe when the church entertained all the members of its area council, was a revelation of the oneness of His Church. The Congolese provided most of the food, much of which was cooked in Mary's kitchen. All she had was held 'for the Master's use'. That time of fellowship will ever be remembered by all who attended. Much was the evidence that the two women working at this place of Bopepe were God's seed corn. Margaret Hayes had gone to do the medical work there and they had worked in well together. A fellow missionary recalled an incident which took place during the visit to Congo of Dr. Sueme, the pastor of Mary's church in Virginia (U.S.A.): "I was invited to stay with Mary during that time and we made visits to the out-churches together in her new car. Pastor Asani was the driver. As we returned one evening from a visit to a plantation we passed a Congolese family on the road. Mother was loaded with a heavy basket on her back, father likewise had baggage and a bunch of spears tied together, and there were three small children. Pastor Asani stopped the car; 'These are our people, we must help them,' he announced. We all got out, and into the back of the car climbed mother, children, and her packages, some of them smelling strongly of dried meat. With difficulty the spears were fixed in the bottom of the car, regardless of the comfort of the passengers. Then everyone packed in and we continued home. It was Mary's car, a new one — a special occasion too, when Pastor Sueme was on a visit, but permission was never asked for the passengers to be taken aboard — all was taken for granted. The party arrived safely and gratefully at Bopepe. What a revelation of the grace of God in His child! Walking with Pastor Sueme that evening I spoke of the incident and remarked that there were many missionaries who were not so Christlike as to allow their property to be used to serve any and everyone without their permission. To me it was another glimpse of the Master, who Himself went about doing good."

In addition to her Bible teaching and general evangelistic work, Miss Baker was also the Mission Treasurer and faithfully managed all field finances. Only a person of exceptional ability could combine so many diverse ministries. She was a close friend of Pastor Asani, the President of the Congo Protestant Council, who also lived at Bopepe, the little village where she worked. Frequently they consulted together and Asani acknowledged his debt to her. In return, she had a real burden for him and the work which God had committed to him. Only a few weeks before she was glorified she wrote to the Rev. J. C. Wright in Ireland.

"Pastor Asani is away at the moment with his family — his wife has been ailing for some time and now he has taken her to the third doctor. We feel that perhaps his having been away so much has made the burden on her with the family too heavy. Do be much in prayer, for more and more Asani is being called away for ministry — all over the Congo, and even further afield, and we thank God for the gift that He has given to Asani, and his great love for the Word and his devotion to the Saviour and the Gospel."

In obedience to the order of the Simbas, Mary, too, made her way to Banalia where she joined the Sharpes and Parrys.

*   *   *

Robina Davidina Gray loved reading and in her early teens became very fond of Pastor Drysdale's Bible work. She was an active member of the Second Dromara Presbyterian Church and was well known in several other Christian fellowships.

After being directed to Mark's Gospel, chapter 16 and verse 15, three times in one day, she realised that this was her call to "go" and applied to Emmanuel Bible College, Birkenhead, for training. On completion of this she realised that a nursing qualification would be very advantageous in her work abroad and therefore studied and obtained her S.R.N. and S.C.M. She was ready to sail for Congo in 1960 but owing to the crisis which followed independence she was unable to go until July 1962. There she was in sole charge of the Government sponsored maternity unit at Bongondza station and was training two Africans in midwifery. She loved the work of evangelism and not only preached to mothers who attended her clinics but frequently went on trek to the local villages. She made several trips to the pygmies bringing them physical relief as well as a message from the Word of Life. "Ruby" was popular wherever she went. In her hometown, during college days, in Belfast City Hospital, where she nursed, and at Bongondza. Her ministry lasted only two years and she was but thirty-four years of age when summoned to Banalia.

*　　　　　*　　　　　*

Thus, Dr. and Mrs. Sharpe and their three children, Mr. and Mrs. Parry and their two children, Miss Mary Baker, Miss "Ruby" Gray and also Miss Margaret Hayes met at Banalia and were "under arrest" together. The full story of Banalia will probably never be told on earth. Days grew into weeks, and weeks became months and still the Mission urged for a relieving party to rescue the saints from the hands of the lions at Banalia and on the 16th December, 1964,

Major Mike Hoare and a party of mercenaries left on this quest. They met fierce opposition outside Stanleyville at a bridge, but after forcing their way across they found no further trace of rebel soldiers.

It was the middle of the wet season and the roads had not been maintained for a considerable while, making the narrow forest roadway both treacherous and dangerous. The creeping growths of vine and tree were trying to reclaim the road for the jungle as the mercenaries' vehicles pushed through towards Banalia. But when they got there they found the town deserted. The streets were empty, the houses were empty, the prison was empty. The mercenaries made their way to the river bank and near to the landing place of the pontoon they found an assortment of clothing which was both torn and blood-stained. There were two sets of women's clothing, three Roman Catholic nuns' habits and one priest's habit, a shirt with a letter to Dr. Sharpe in the breast pocket, two pairs of children's jeans and one tee-shirt belonging to Grace and Andrew Parry, two shirts with a "Made in England" label on them, one having a letter addressed to an African in the pocket, four separate shoes, two women's, one child's and one indeterminate, Miss Baker's passport, Mr. Parry's driving licence, Dr. and Mrs. Sharpe's identity cards and private papers and Miss Gray's identity card and Bible. The sight brought tears to the eyes of the hardened rescuers for they could only imagine the last hours of anguish suffered by the gallant band of missionaries. The last walk to the river bank must have been dreadful to behold as the party were led forth to be killed. Those at Banalia experienced both a Gethsemane and Calvary and after the hours of anguish when men, women and children were slain, they entered their heavenly home. The nightmare of the ferry pathway led the gallant group to "the way of holiness".

As Isaiah promised to those who conquer it: "No lion shall be there, nor any ravenous beast shall go up thereon, it shall not be found there; but the redeemed shall walk there; and the ransomed of the Lord shall return, and come to Zion with songs and everlasting joy upon their heads; they shall obtain joy and gladness, and sorrow and sighing shall flee away" (Isaiah 35, vs. 9 and 10).

CHAPTER THIRTEEN

HERSELF SHE COULD NOT SAVE

LAUREL KATHLEEN MCCALLUM came from Perth in Western Australia and was a graduate of the Perth Bible Institute. She first sailed for Congo in 1946 when she met Thelma Wild from Canada (later Mrs. Thelma Southard), and after prayer they asked the Field Council for an assignment together. They were both born pioneers and they found an area in the forest which had never enjoyed the ministry of a Christian missionary. They built a small leaf shack and made furniture from packing cases. Those early years were spent in pioneer and evangelistic work, particularly amongst women and children. After a while Laurel moved to Wanie Rukula which was then a new station and was led by the Rev. and Mrs. G. Kerrigan. Again Laurel set herself the task of winning women and children to Christ and not only spent many hours visiting the little mud and wattle dwellings but also conducted a day school for girls. Her deep devotion to the Lord and ardent spirit soon reached the souls of many of the children under her care and she had the joy of leading many to Christ. Wanie Rukula was a hard and primitive place and the infantile mortality rate was high. Not only babies died but very often mothers died during childbirth or immediately after. Laurel developed a real burden for helpless and unwanted children and began caring for those left motherless. Very often they were nurtured for a few weeks on the juice from sugar cane or other similar impossible baby foods until there was only a breath of life left in them and they were often but a bag of bones and sores when they were carried to the missionary

for help. Lovingly, Laurel received them into her home and
cared for them day and night. Sometimes the little scrap of
life looked so pitiful and the task of rearing it so impossible
that, yes, the thought was there, even the missionaries thought
it might be better to let the little thing slip away. But Laurel
never felt like that. With a heart flowing over with pity and
devotion to the Master's service she took the infant in and
cared for it with the utmost dedication. Sometimes she
would have three or four such children by her bed and as
soon as she had fed one and put it down to sleep and got
back into bed herself so another would wake and start crying.
She was never too tired to tend to them and often would be
up more hours of the night than she slept, boiling water
and making milk from powder, sometimes rocking one off
to sleep, sometimes crooning over them. If the nights were
cold and she had not sufficient blankets in her home she
tore up her own clothing to cover them. Each evening they
gathered around her knee and she taught them choruses and
Bible verses and then told them a Bible story followed by
prayers. And so her family grew, both physically and numeri-
cally. By 1964 she had more than eighty children in her
kindergarten and even though they were well cared for, they
were not spoiled. "Now, you kids, will you be quiet," she
would cry at the top of her voice, sometimes in English and
sometimes in Swahili. "Go outside and play," and out they
would go. Presently one would come in, lisping, "Mulk,
Mama, Mulk," and patiently she would make the child a
glass of milk and hold it for the little one to drink, then a
kiss on the forehead and "Now, run away and play and be
a good girl," and off the child would run knowing that "mama"
loved her. The children came from all sorts of conditions
and for varied reasons.

Colette's mother died shortly after she was born and
immediately death wails echoed through the village. Pan-
demonium broke out and the unfortunate husband was
seized by the dead mother's relatives and dragged away.
They attempted to cut his throat and almost succeeded but

he was rescued by his own relatives and the huge gash in his throat was stitched in hospital. Thus, baby Colette was left both motherless and fatherless and for five months her grandmother did her very best to look after her. She was more intelligent than most women of her age and fortunately she managed to obtain a feeding bottle and some powdered milk. However she knew nothing of hygiene and it was amazing that the child survived. After a few months of nothing but powdered milk it grew weaker and weaker and contracted dysentery. Almost on the point of death Colette was brought to the missionary for help. Laurel took her in, saved her life and she grew to be a happy child, full of life and finding plenty of mischief. Laurel often took Colette to see her father and other relatives who remained pagans, but the miracle of the saved life remained a constant reminder to them of the power of Laurel's God and she never lost an opportunity to tell them of the Saviour's love.

Another child was named Machosi, which means 'Tears'. She was born in the depths of the forest at a hunting camp in a leaf shack. Her mother was very young, and died two days after giving birth to her first child and thus Machosi found a name. The father was unable to raise the child himself and none of his relatives were inclined to help him, but he knew of one person who would help however desperate was the need. So he brought Machosi to Laurel, who readily received her and Laurel became her mother and the child gained weight and grew steadily. Then, one day, illness struck the child and Machosi got weaker at an alarming rate. Laurel turned to her medicines and did all she could to arrest the progress of the disease. After twelve days Machosi was extremely weak and as Laurel massaged her whole body with olive oil she realised she was beyond the help of medicine. She wrapped the child in a sheet and took her into her bedroom and laid her on her bed. Laurel dropped to her knees and more tears were shed, only this time from the missionary's eyes. Claiming the promise of restoration in James 5 she read the passage from her Bible and asked the Lord to inter-

vene and heal the child. After pouring out her heart in prayer
she went to rest and the next morning saw her prayers
answered. The crisis passed and Machosi began to regain her
strength and she soon recovered completely. Then came
Yisaka.

Yisaka's father knew nothing about child care or feeding
and therefore he did practically nothing! His five-and-a-half
month old baby boy was neglected for nearly four weeks,
ever since his mother died, and then when the condition of the
baby was serious indeed he went to Laurel to plead for help.
Laurel took Yisaka in and as she held him in her arms she
wondered if it would be possible for this little infant to live.
She turned to the Lord for help and guidance. Using a pipette,
a drop of heated water containing a small quantity of con-
densed milk was put into the babe's mouth and as soon as
it found the warm liquid it made an attempt to suck. This
sign of life greatly encouraged Laurel. For the next forty-eight
hours, day and night, the child was given a few drops of
nourishment with the pipette until he was strong enough
to take nourishment from a bottle. To keep the little mite
alive was a full-time job as it took thirty minutes to help it
to take two ounces of milk and one and a half hours to get
it comfortable afterwards, and then it was time for the next
feed. This curtailed Laurel's village evangelism. One day,
feeling this keenly and wondering what she should do, she
picked up *Daily Light*. The first verse for the day was, "Take
this child and nurse it for Me and I will give thee thy wages".
God had answered, she was doing His will and soon she
began to collect her wages! The baby's uncle, who had
been most hostile to the Gospel, came to the Lord. Yisaka's
father was converted and when Laurel was able to restart
her school twelve boys and eighteen girls attended. Once
a month Laurel took this group to the village to spend the
weekend in witnessing. Several of the children professed the
Lord Jesus as Saviour. Later Yisaka's step-mother also came
to the Lord.

In the crisis which followed Independence in 1960 Laurel was faced with a problem. If she evacuated who would care for her little children? And so she remained at her post. She was never harmed throughout those days and her children were never neglected.

The last letter received from Miss McCallum in the Australian Home Office was dated July 26th, 1964. It was typical of her letters, expressing deep concern and compassion for those amongst whom she was working, rejoicing in victories won, full of hope and confidence for the future and tinged with sorrow for the sudden death of the little girl she had mothered for three years.

"Last week," she wrote, "Mamaya Paskau, the old leper woman, went to be with the Lord. One rejoices unreservedly in her Homegoing. A soul set at liberty from her disease-ridden body to enter into the joy and glory of the Lord, and in the resurrection to receive a new glorious body... O what a wonderful hope is ours in Christ. Even in the pain of losing a precious little child from one's side there is the hope, the joy of the certainty of reunion in the glory where there is no more parting, sickness or pain. How precious our Saviour's love."

In her last prayer bulletin, dated May, 1964, Miss McCallum wrote, "We and the African Church need your intercession more now than maybe ever before. As you have all heard, there are subversive forces at work throughout the whole country. In some places they feel they have attained sufficient power to attack; in others they are still gathering their forces. Pray that, if the Lord pleases, the door may be kept open to the spread of the Gospel. Pray too, that the Church will be true and grow to His glory where and when persecution arises. There have been those who have died as Stephen died, and we praise the Lord for them."

Laurel's love in the Lord and zeal won her way into the hearts and confidence of all at Maganga and Wanie Rukula and it was this love which conquered when the preaching of others failed. Laurel erected her own memorial in Congo.

It is a living memorial of scores of Congolese children who have been saved by her devotion and who are now growing up as instructed Christians prepared to continue in the work that was so dear to her heart and living the life which she lived to the fullest. In spite of her having saved so many African lives, when she was led to the river bank for execution herself she could not save.

CHAPTER FOURTEEN

THE WAY OF SORROWS

THE TRAVELLING FISH SHOP was a familiar sight in Blackpool and the cheerful disposition of the fish salesman won him many friends as well as maintaining a reasonable business. In 1927, on the death of his father, John Arton took over the motorcycle and converted sidecar and went into the fish business. John Arton was born on the 16th June, 1909, and lived in the Layton district of Blackpool and studied at the Palatine school. In the centre of the Queenstown area of Blackpool was the Queenstown Mission Hall, standing as a radiant light to the poorer classes who lived in the tenement buildings or tumbledown cottages. John's grandfather was actually one of the founders of this Hall and it was here that John attended Sunday school and later became a teacher and a member of the choir. He loved singing and his strong bass voice led the remainder in the well-known Gospel hymns and choruses or modulated to fit in with the harmonies of the choir. Week by week John listened to the Gospel story expounded by faithful missioners or laymen and these messages provided the foundation of his faith and brought him to the Cross of Christ. The missioners' burden for souls became his, and while he travelled from place to place selling fish the Spirit of God moved him to dedicate his life to become a "fisher of men". By the early nineteen-thirties John was both Sunday school superintendent and president of the mission council and it was with some surprise that his co-workers learned that he was going into training and to the mission field. His work and organising ability at Blackpool will be remembered and his enthusiasm for evangelistic work and powerful preaching made an indelible mark on the town. However, he willingly left Blackpool and commenced training at All Nations Missionary College. Owing to the outbreak of war in 1939 his studies were interrupted and he returned home and resumed work at Queenstown Mission. He joined the A.R.P. and in 1940 qualified as a first-aider and eventually became a full time member of the St. John's Ambulance Brigade stationed in Blackpool under the Civil Defence Authority. He sailed to Congo in 1945 and worked as a village evangelist.

Only eighty miles from Blackpool in the city of Leeds a young lady named Betty Ingleson also responded to the call of God to foreign fields and first of all qualified as a nurse. She trained in Preston and soon qualified as a Ward Sister, after which she went to Mount Hermon Missionary Training College. John and Betty met in Congo for the first time and soon felt that the Lord had brought them together and they were to go forward in His service as man and wife. They were married in the Mission Church at Boyulu on the 30th September, 1946. The medical skill of Betty Arton soon received wide acknowledgment. While she practised at Boyulu it was not unususal for white people to pass the European doctor at Bafwasende, four miles away, and consult her about their ailments. Africans coveted her services, particularly to deliver a baby and, in addition, Mrs. Arton had a special burden for the neglected and ostracised lepers. She never ceased to campaign on their behalf and try to bring a measure of relief to them. God gave them a daughter in 1948 whom they named Heather Evelyn, but she was unfortunately delicate from the beginning and only weighed 2¼ pounds at birth. She became very ill prior to the 1960 crisis and was flown home in an oxygen tent. The serious nature of her illness caused her parents grave anxiety but at such a time as this the devotion of Christian friends was stirred and prayer meetings commenced throughout the land. One such prayer meeting was started at Clarendon School in Abergele, North Wales, where she was due to begin her secondary education. For nearly two terms the staff prayer meeting brought the needs of an

Miss Laurel Kathleen McCallum.
(see chapter 13)

Miss McCallum with baby Colette.

Miss McCallum and some of the children
for whom she cared.

Photo : Donovan C. W

Top—Mr. and Mrs. John Arton and Heather.

Above—Miss Jean Sweet.

Above right—Mr. Chester Burk.

Right—Mr. and Mrs. Chester Burk visit a Congolese home, inviting all to come to a meeting.

unknown child to the Throne of Grace and she was restored
to health. She eventually arrived at Clarendon in 1961 and
not only looked delicate but was much smaller than other
children of her age. However, she was popular in her form
and was soon affectionately known as "flea", and "flea"
remained her school nickname. But she concentrated on her
lessons and set her mind on becoming a nurse like her mother
and was successful in passing several subjects in the General
Certificate of Education in the summer of 1964. Heather
did not have many close friends and never spoke to anyone
of a definite experience of conversion, but her life clearly
indicated she belonged to the Lord and nobody ever questioned
it. Various friends, together with their church at Preston,
made it possible for Heather to visit her parents during the
school holidays in 1964 and thus she was trapped with her
parents at Boyulu.

The Artons were evangelists; whatever else they did was
only a "make-weight" to their main task of evangelism.

John had a battery-powered projector and a large selection
of colour slides, which were exceptionally popular with the
Congolese. Skilfully John would unfold a Bible story, cap-
tivating his congregation, and would hold them in breathless
silence as he made his appeal. During the time of "house
arrest" John undertook to give Bible readings to the group,
and based his expositions on the Book of Revelation. His
spiritual perception and understanding were an uplift to the
party at Boyulu as they relived the days of Emperor anti-
christs, and were constantly reminded that ultimate victory
is in the hand of God.

*   *   *

Jean Elizabeth Sweet was converted whilst at Teacher
Training College in London. During her years of teaching
she was able to run a Christian Union in the school through
which she gained the esteem and respect of her fellow members
of staff and had the joy of leading some of the children to

the Saviour. In 1958 she felt the call to a wider sphere of
service and after studying at Redcliffe Missionary Training
College, she was accepted for overseas service by U.F.M.
Owing to the crisis in Congo following Independence she was
unable to leave immediately but, feeling the impelling call of
God, waited patiently until the way opened in August, 1962.
Before she left she designed her prayer card and selected two
verses of Scripture to leave with those who had promised
to pray for her and the work she was undertaking: "For I am
persuaded that neither death, nor life, nor angels, nor princi-
palities, nor powers, nor things present, nor things to come,
nor height, nor depth, nor any other creature shall be able
to separate us from the love of God which is in Christ Jesus
our Lord" (Romans 8, vs. 38-39). Little could she have realised
then that she was to prove those verses to the uttermost
only two years later. On arrival in Congo she was appointed
to teach in the Teachers' Training School at Ekoko, special-
ising in mathematics, where she spent two very happy years.
In addition to her teaching schedule she helped with the girls'
youth work and ran a Sunday school for the children of
leprosy patients. When the term finished in June 1964, Jean
went to Boyulu to spend the vacation with a fellow missionary,
Miss Olive McCarten, who had been her inseparable companion since college days. Here she spent a time of rest and
wrote a large number of letters to friends and supporters
before she was trapped a month later by the invading rebel
forces. She wrote to one of her supporters:

"At present I am staying with a friend at Boyulu, another of
our stations, and enjoying the time very much. I expect to return
to Ekoko about August 10th.

School finished on June 24th when the ten fourth year students
received their certificates — they will be teaching in the primary
schools now. They certainly need our prayers for they face many
temptations. We start again on September 4th when we expect to
take thirty-six new students into the first year. This is a real answer
to prayer because at one time it looked as though we would have

to open without a first year owing to lack of staff (three of our missionaries will be on furlough), but the Lord has undertaken and other missionaries have been designated to Ekoko.

We had a very happy Spiritual Life Conference for a week at the beginning of July when between seventy and eighty pastors and evangelists came on to the station. It proved a great blessing to us all. These folk are really hungry for the Word, which is encouraging in a land where there is so much unrest.

Starting on August 17th we are holding a week's refresher course for the Primary School teachers. This is a new venture and we would value your prayers."

* * *

Mr. Chester Burk, although born in the United States of America, was a Canadian citizen and lived in Sundre, Alberta. He was quiet, solid and steady, and yet was a tremendous preacher of the Word and loved to teach deeper things of God. He always had the apt illustration which fixed his messages in the hearts of his hearers. His building techniques and ability to repair broken down trucks were exceptional and greatly appreciated by Congolese and missionary alike. In spite of a very serious illness which preceded his last furlough and an eye infection of his wife, they insisted upon returning to Congo during 1964 and before leaving the homeland he testified:

"The very word 'missionary' always held a strange attraction for me, and as long as I can remember I have had an interest in Africa. The first time I saw slides of missionary work in that land, the Spirit of God spoke to my heart about serving Him there. I was, however, hesitant and fearful about the Bible School training necessary.

I was married and had settled down on a farm. I tried to make myself believe that this was God's place for me, but His Spirit gave me no rest. I was afraid of men's faces and had a natural aversion to becoming a preacher. In God's providence I was brought face to face with death and delivered in answer to prayer. It was then that the full force of 1 Cor. 6, vs. 19, 20: 'What? know

ye not that your body is the temple of the Holy Ghost which is
in you, which ye have of God, and ye are not your own? For ye
are bought with a price: therefore glorify God in your body and
in your spirit which are God's', came home to my heart and I
put my hand to the plough — not to look back".

*   *   *

On August 7th the first truckloads of rebel soldiers arrived
at Boyulu and began terrorising the town, making the mission
station a focal point for their activities. Day or night the
little group of God's servants, including Mr. and Mrs. Arton
and Heather, Mr. and Mrs. Burk, Miss Jean Sweet, Miss
Laurel McCallum, Miss Olive McCarten and Miss Louie
Rimmer, never knew when they would be ordered out of their
house at the point of a gun or marched around in their house
with the muzzle of a gun in their backs. Time after time
the rebels searched the house looking for firearms, transmitters, food or valuables. Several times Chester repaired
their trucks and welded parts of their cars without any thanks
and by November vehicles, typewriters, tape recorders
and all other valuables had been taken, with the exception
of a small radio receiver which Miss McCarten managed to
conceal in a sugar box. On November 24th, the day of the
Belgian parachute drop, they were taken by trucks to Bafwasende about four miles away, and were put in a small room in
an empty house, together with eighteen Roman Catholic
missionaries. The floor of the room was covered with dirty
and foul smelling water, there was no ventilation, and there
was an open toilet in an adjoining compartment. There was
not sufficient room for them all to lie down. Their watches,
spectacles and shoes were then taken. During the next three
days they were mercilessly knocked around and once they
were paraded through the streets almost naked while the
Congolese jeered at them and hurled abuses. On Friday,
November 27th, an angry crowd of fleeing rebels arrived
from Stanleyville and stirred up the passions of their com-
panions. Everyone was ordered outside the house and told

that they were going to be killed. First the men were marched towards the river bank and a volley of shots was heard in the distance. The ladies were split into three groups. Miss Rimmer, Miss McCarten and Mrs. Burk were in the first group, the Roman Catholic sisters in the second, and Mrs. Arton and Heather, Miss McCallum and Miss Sweet in the third. The first group was ordered to march toward the river bank. Suddenly the Simba in charge of the group ordered them to turn around and they were marched back toward their room. They passed Mrs. Arton and Heather, Miss McCallum and Miss Sweet, who were making their way toward the river. At the last moment the rebel colonel ordered Heather to the other party, intending to spare her life, but she clung to her mother. Then the Catholic sisters "got into a huddle". Gripping each other firmly round the waist and with heads bowed forward they formed a solid circle of humanity and just refused to move. The soldiers shouted at them, cursed them and struck them, but still they maintained their resistance. Miss McCarten, Miss Rimmer and Mrs. Burk who were in the same group as the nuns, looked on in fear and trembling, wondering what the outcome was to be. They looked toward the river bank and saw Mrs. Arton and Heather, Miss McCallum and Miss Sweet slowly making their way along the tree-lined road, their shoeless feet knocking against the rocks in the way. They could not but help think of their Master who also had experienced the mocking and the spitting, and had made His way along the "Way of Sorrows", first lined with eastern houses and then up the green hill outside the city. He, too, had laid down His life for those whom He loved and was buried in a nameless grave. Miss McCarten and her colleagues never saw the others again and could only assume that the river bank at Bafwasende was their Calvary and the waters of the River Lindi their nameless grave. Even from the point where they were standing they could hear the water tirelessly moving along its course, tearing at the stones and tree stumps which tried to impede it and contemplated that these waters in which so many had been baptised in the name of the Father, Son and Holy Spirit, symbolising the new life that they had found in Christ, continued on their way murmuring their eternal promise, "they shall rise again!" After a while, the Simbas tired of trying to move the nuns, and the party was ordered back to the house. Mrs. Dolena Burk asked where her husband was, to which they replied that he had been killed. Later, however, they denied this and said he had been taken to a Catholic station a few miles away. A day or two later the story was again reversed and every time they saw another soldier they were given a different story. The arrival of the Catholic priest from the station where the other missionaries were supposed to have been taken, destroyed any hope that remained.

On the day following the massacre, the fourteen survivors were ordered from their humble room and were marched in the merciless sun a distance of three miles to a neighbouring village, where they were hidden in a small native hut, where the Simbas hoped they could not be found. They were guarded constantly day and night and were thrown upon the mercy of the Lord. Prayer became vital and the promise of His presence real. For three weeks they managed to survive under these appalling conditions and even avoided contracting fever and disease in spite of the fact that they had no option but to drink unfiltered and unboiled water. One night, one of the survivors overheard a group of rebels talking and silently she listened, straining her ears for every word which might give a clue to the fate of the others. The execution of the whites at Bafwasende was the subject of conversation and it seemed that the men had been shot and the women speared to death. Day followed day and they wondered what the outcome would be. News was unobtainable and rumours abounded. One thing was certain, they could not continue indefinitely as they were, and they wondered if the mercenaries would ever find them in their village prison and, if they did, would they be humiliated and suffer even within sight of rescue? After three weeks of physical

and mental torture they suddenly heard the sound of guns
blazing and heavy vehicles approaching, and they realised
that the troops were on their way. They ran to the window to
see a convoy of vehicles manned by white troops with guns
raining lead on the houses and shooting anyone who came
into sight. Their guards fled but, as they feared, the mercenaries
drove right past. In the distance they heard the town of
Bafwasende being raked with gunfire and from the noise it
sounded as though a major battle was being fought. Just as
they were debating on the best course of action one of their
guards returned and signalled to the three ladies to follow
him, leaving the nuns in the house. They went to the edge
of the forest and the guard told them to crouch down. What
was in store for them now? Were they to die within sight of the
rescuers? What plan was afoot? The Simba came and
crouched in the grass beside them. Slowly he began talking,
"Do not fear, I am not going to kill you. I expect you are
wondering why I am going to save you. I will tell you. I was
brought up in a Protestant school. I have saved you. Now
you save me! Soon your friends will return and we will go
to meet them." So this was his plan. He had spared their
lives and now they were to bargain for his. It seemed like
a miracle, but before they could even appreciate it a rebel
officer came in sight and approached them. A cruel smile
crept over his face as he saw the three missionaries crouching
in the grass. He took his gun from his shoulder and loaded
it in front of them. He raised it in their direction and they
caught a glimpse of his blood-shot eyes and thought that
the end had now come. Olive McCarten bowed her head and
prayed as she had never prayed before and from the distance
she heard the gunfire becoming louder and wondered if the
mercenaries were on their way back. She dared scarcely
open her eyes. What was the officer doing? Taking aim,
preparing to shoot? No! Suddenly and for no apparent
reason he slung the gun on his shoulder again and walked
off into the bush. They rushed from their hiding place and
on to the road. The mercenaries, who had almost given up

hope of finding anyone alive and were preparing to return to Stanleyville with the passports belonging to Mr. and Mrs. Arton and Heather, which they had found in the headquarters of the rebels, saw these ladies approaching them sheltering a frightened Simba. Several white soldiers jumped from their vehicles and ran to shake hands. The ladies found that words were just impossible. They, too, could only shake hands and look at their rescuers. One came forward and acted as spokesman, "Please accept our apologies, ladies, for our appearance. Major Hoare has not provided us with shaving water for several days!"

Olive assured them there was no need to apologise and told them she thought they were the best looking lot of white men she had seen for a long time. The nuns, now free too, expressed their thanks, using Olive as interpreter. They went to the Catholic Mission and had a drink, after which the mercenaries took them to an open space outside Bafwasende and radioed for a helicopter. They were flown to Stanleyville and the next day on to Leopoldville. Then from the dust and the heat of the tropics they were flown towards Britain. The journey was slow, for official offices were closed, aeroplane and train services had been cut, for the world was on holiday! It was Christmas, it was the time when the world was remembering the coming of the Christ Child and His message of peace on earth and good will to all men. Yet still they managed to reach home and arrived at Victoria Station, London, on the eve of Christmas Day and those from Britain were united with their loved ones.

CHAPTER FIFTEEN

THE LEAP OF THE LION

NEVER BEFORE had the members of the Body of Christ undergone such a severe testing in the Oriental Province of North East Congo. The leading U.F.M. pastor and President of the Congo Protestant Council, Asani Benedict, was at Oicha when the rebellion broke out. His wife had been unwell for a considerable time and he felt it necessary to consult a doctor at the A.I.M. Oicha hospital. Altogether twelve U.F.M. workers visited Oicha, including Asani himself and Yokana Jean, the Director of Education. If they had been in their home towns they would almost certainly have been slain. When the rebels reached Oicha they raided the hospital, but those who were around fled for their lives, narrowly escaping death. Asani led his party into the forest. He felt it better to abandon Mary Baker's car which he had borrowed, and risk a back road to the Uganda border. Oicha was left in ruins and with many dead along the streets. It took the gallant party ten days to walk to the border and then they sought refuge with the Anglican workers who graciously found them accommodation. Asani and his party were distressed indeed when they heard that so many of their beloved missionary co-workers had been glorified and wrote:

"May the Lord grant strength to the families who are going through this trial and for whom we are praying and to whom we express our profound sympathy.

It is impossible to understand why God has permitted these catastrophies to come to our country and the seeming deliverance of His servants into the hands of the enemy; but we cannot dispute with God, for He knows all and will re-establish peace and stability in the Congo according to His perfect will.

We believe that these trials will reinforce our solidarity to better accomplish the noble task which the Lord has entrusted to us. We share with you all the pain which you have suffered because of the name of Jesus Christ, the name which you brought to us.

In the name of the Evangelical Church of Upper Congo, we express our sympathy to all the missionaries who passed through the trial and our Christian greetings to all our brothers and sisters in Christ."

The number of pastors, evangelists, teachers and elders who also have laid down their lives for the sake of the Cross may never be known. Many societies, organisations and individuals paid their tributes to those of whom "the world was not worthy".

The secretaries of the various societies who had suffered loss in Congo felt it desirable to hold a united memorial service in London and thus, under the auspices of the Evangelical Missionary Alliance, a service of thanksgiving, remembrance and prayer was called on Saturday, 6th February, 1965 at Westminster Chapel, Buckingham Gate, London, S.W.1. The large chapel was packed to capacity as well as two overflow meetings, the total attendance being approximately 3,200. The Secretary of the E.M.A., Rev. Gilbert W. Kirby, led the service and testimonies were given by Rev. H. Jenkinson (U.F.M.), Miss Doreen West (B.M.S.), Mr. Jack Scholes (W.E.C.), Miss Kathleen Lucas (Assemblies of God). Pastor Georges Tomatala, a Congolese national pastor, then paid tribute to those who rested from their labours. This was followed by the Act of Remembrance conducted by the Rev. Leonard F. Harris, General Secretary of the Unevangelized Fields Mission. Leonard Harris himself had spent the best years of his life as a missionary, having sailed for Brazil in 1922. He was a worker of the highest spiritual calibre and gave hinself for those who were lost in the darkness of paganism. God had honoured his ministry with remarkable demonstrations of divine power and sometimes the whole congregation of a church had waited in breathless silence for him to finish speaking as the Spirit stirred the depths of their souls. He was appointed field leader and skilfully directed the advance of the work. Leonard Harris returned to the homeland after World War II and became General Secretary. Under his experienced counsel and powerful preaching the Mission then grew rapidly. He became a leading missionary preacher and one of the most prominent missionary statesmen of the twentieth century. Mr. Harris commenced the Act of Remembrance by quoting a letter received from the Rev. G. A. Scott, of the China Inland Mission, recounting their experience during the Boxer Rising in 1900:

"Again and again our minds go back to those days of similar suspense in China in 1900. Some were taken, others were left. Much of the work seemed to be collapsing and our magazine is peppered with such headlines as 'Rebellion at Yuhshan', 'The Riot at Sihwa'. One whole issue was given up to a memorial number for those who had suffered martyrdom and yet one notices right at the forefront of such a publication, the triumphant words 'The Lord Reigneth'. It would appear that adults and children who laid down their lives in the dangerous days in China numbered one hundred and eighty-seven, fifty-eight men and seventy women being the adults. Yet the significant thing about these old records is this; no one took his hand from the plough, unless God had removed it, and even during that year of tragedy and suffering, twenty-two fresh workers arrived in China in connection with the Mission.

In one of the Editorial notes open on the desk in front of me, I read these words, 'The husbandman does not mourn over the death of the seed he has sown, nay, rather he rejoices in hope of an abundant harvest. Then let us also lift up our heads and rejoice. The living seed, not only of the Word of God, but of precious lives laid down, has been sown more widely and in greater measure than ever before in China, and though the harvest wait, it will surely be reaped — and reaped abundantly'."

Mr. Harris then went on to say that not only were the conditions similar to those during the Boxer Rising but also the experiences of the Mission, for U.F.M. and W.E.C. both had received applications from young people to serve in Congo and some had, in fact, arrived after the news of the rising. God has never lacked men and women willing to face danger and privation for Christ's sake and the present situation in Congo was no exception. He asked the congregation to stand while he read the names of those who were glorified or missing:

KNOWN TO BE KILLED

CHESTER BURK
　　　　　Unevangelized Fields Mission　　　　　(*Canada*)

PAUL CARLSON
　　　　　Evangelical Mission Covenant Church　(*U.S.A.*)

IRENE FERRELL
　　　　　Congo Inland Mission　　　　　　　　(*U.S.A.*)

MURIEL HARMAN
　　　　　Worldwide Evangelization Crusade　　(*Canada*)

BURLEIGH LAW
　　　　　Central Congo Methodist Mission　　　(*U.S.A.*)

WILLIAM MCCHESNEY
　　　　　Worldwide Evangelization Crusade　　(*U.S.A.*)

HECTOR MCMILLAN
　　　　　Unevangelized Fields Mission　　　　　(*Canada*)

PHYLLIS RINE
　　　　　Africa Christian Mission　　　　　　　(*U.S.A.*)

JAMES RODGER
　　　　　Worldwide Evangelization Crusade

CYRIL TAYLOR
　　　　　Worldwide Evangelization Crusade　　(*New Zealand*)

JOSEPH WALTER TUCKER
　　　　　Assemblies of God　　　　　　　　　(*U.S.A.*)

DIED IN PRISON

WILLIAM SCHOLTEN
Unevangelized Fields Mission   (*U.S.A.*)

KILLED IN 1960

EDMUND HODGSON
Congo Evangelistic Mission
ELTON KNAUF
Congo Evangelistic Mission

MISSING, PRESUMED KILLED

JOHN ARTON
Unevangelized Fields Mission
ELIZABETH ARTON
Unevangelized Fields Mission
HEATHER ARTON
MARY BAKER
Unevangelized Fields Mission   (*U.S.A.*)
ROBINA D. GRAY
Unevangelized Fields Mission
MARGARET HAYES
Unevangelized Fields Mission
LAUREL K. MCCALLUM
Unevangelized Fields Mission   (*Australia*)
DENNIS E. PARRY
Unevangelized Fields Mission
NORA M. PARRY
Unevangelized Fields Mission
ANDREW PARRY
GRACE PARRY

IAN M. SHARPE
    Unevangelized Fields Mission

AUDREY M. SHARPE
    Unevangelized Fields Mission

JILLIAN SHARPE

ALISON SHARPE

ANDREW SHARPE

JEAN E. SWEET
    Unevangelized Fields Mission

MISSING

WINIFRED DAVIES
    Worldwide Evangelization Crusade

and concluded by quoting Bishop Howe's immortal hymn:

> "But, lo! there breaks a yet more glorious day;
> The saints triumphant rise in bright array;
> The King of Glory passes on His way,
>   Hallelujah!
>
> From earth's wide bounds, from ocean's farthest
>   coast
> Through gates of pearl streams in the countless host
> Singing to Father, Son and Holy Ghost,
>   Hallelujah!

Mr. Leonard Moules, General Secretary of the Worldwide Evangelisation Crusade, then gave the address and, basing his remarks on Revelation 6, verse 11: "And white robes were given unto every one of them; and it was said unto them, that they should rest yet for a little season, until their fellow servants also and their brethren, that should be killed as they were, should be fulfilled", said that "Congo" is no accident. A pruning is necessary to bring forth fruit. Sometimes it takes death to hew the rock-face of apathy in the Church before the needs of finance and personnel are met.

God was making up His number during the Simba rising
and he felt sure that the death of the saints would act as a
stimulant to the Church at home and hereafter His work
would be speeded abroad. The mighty congregation sat
strangely silent while the Lord's servant was speaking and
then rose to make the chapel re-echo with the strains of
the triumphant hymn:

> "Crown Him with many crowns,
> The Lamb upon His throne;
> Hark! how the heavenly anthem drowns
> All music but its own."

How strange that it needs a tragedy to awaken God's people
to action! Yet even more mysterious is the fact that it has
always been so since the early days when God began revealing
Himself to mankind. In the 13th chapter of I Kings is the
record of the old prophet of Bethel. He was not necessarily
old in years but old in spirit, in fact he had grown cold and
had become lethargic. The voice that had once spoken the
words of God was silenced and the hands that had once
offered sacrifice at His altar no longer served. But God had
work to do and when His old servant failed He appointed
a new one. The sons of the old prophet ran to him and told
him that a young prophet from Judah was offering sacrifice
in his place and the old prophet's mind filled with anger
and bitterness and he went out to find the young prophet
and discovered him sitting under an oak tree and invited
him home to eat and drink. At first the young prophet refused
saying, "It was said to him by the Word of the Lord, thou
shalt eat no bread nor drink water there, nor turn again to
go by the way that thou camest". But the old prophet lied
to him and deceived him and told him that he had received
a subsequent revelation of divine guidance, and that he was
to go home and eat and the young prophet was led into the
way of disobedience, and when he resumed his journey "A lion
met him by the way and slew him and his carcase was cast
in the way and the ass stood by it, the lion also stood by

the carcase" (I Kings 13, verse 24). When the news was carried
to the old prophet of Bethel he was shaken to the depths of
his soul when he realised what a tragedy his actions had
caused and he was convicted of his apathy which had spoilt
his life, and God turned the tragedy to triumph in His own
way. Tears of repentance flowed from the eyes of the old
prophet and he spoke to his sons saying, "When I am dead,
then bury me in the sepulchre wherein the man of God is
buried, lay my bones beside his bones". Thus a breath of
revival blew through that household at Bethel and the work
of God again became vital. *The leap of a lion changed the
spiritual destiny of the people.*

In the early days of the Mission three valiant pioneers
were murdered on their way to reach the Kayapo Indians
for Christ. One of them, Mr. Fred Wright, in a last letter
to his prayer partners, wrote:

"As far as we can ascertain, the Kayapos are very numerous.
We are quite aware that humanly speaking, we are as good as dead
men, but brethren, stand by us as one man. Do not criticize. We
are beyond criticism as we go forward in the name of the Lord
and under His command, after having fully counted the cost.

Finally, it is well to remember that Calvary was and is the
greatest victory of all times. Death to the Christian is not defeat.
Should the Lord will that we be taken, our prayer is that more
men and more money be rushed out to follow up this advance.
Let our generalship be greater than that of our arch-enemy, the
devil, and set aside all sentiment for the sake of the spread of the
Gospel of our Lord Jesus Christ in this our day".

The news of the martyrdom of the three Freds shook the
then young Mission as it did the Christian public who had
seen them go forth on their task. The three Freds had counted
the cost and left all that they had to those who should follow
in their train and take up the work of bringing the Gospel
to the Kayapos after them. The Mission launched a Memorial
Fund, announcing to the public, in faith, "We feel that the

Mr. John Arton is assisted by two Congolese in preparing wood for a new building.

Mr. Yokana Jean (left) Director of the U.F.M. educational work, and Pastor Asani Benedict, leading pastor of the U.F.M. national Church. They escaped to Uganda during the rising.

The well-designed and well-built church at Boyulu which is packed to capacity every Sunday.

Miss Margaret Hayes.
(see chapter 16)

Wither Congo?

THE LEAP OF THE LION

death of these three young men is a challenge to us to go forward . . . our job will be to send out men who shall take the place of those who have laid down their lives", and not only the money but also the men came forward. In fact, the U.F.M. missionaries have worked among the Kayapos for over thirty years and have rejoiced to see the first members of the Kayapo tribe join the ranks of those redeemed by the blood of Christ.

In 1964 the "lions" leapt upon twenty-eight servants of God in Congo. They gained the Crowns of Life and by their sagas lit the fires of intercession on behalf of Congo and assured the triumph of the Cross in the coming days.

CHAPTER SIXTEEN

NO WAY BACK

IT IS SELDOM that one with such a handicap as Margaret Hayes' ever has the grit and stamina needed to overcome it and eventually be accepted for missionary service. Margaret was born with a speech impediment which could not be corrected, but in spite of this she concentrated at study and passed both her S.R.N. and S.C.M. examinations, then obtained her tropical medicine diploma in French, and eventually learned the Bangala tongue so that she could speak to the people of Congo in the vernacular.

Margaret was educated at Barnsbury Central School for Girls, London, N.1, and during a convention felt compelled by the Holy Spirit to offer for missionary service, which she did only six weeks later. While she was studying the French language and nursing in Belgium she became acquainted with a Miss Alice Styles. They frequently spoke together of their spiritual pilgrimage, and on one occasion Margaret opened her heart and said, "I cannot understand it at all, but I'll have to go on, because there's no way back". Miss Styles was strangely moved by these words and that night, the 22nd January, 1957, sat in her room and wrote a poem which she dedicated to her gallant missionary colleague, Margaret Hayes:

> *"I did not know the way would prove so steep;*
> *That there would be such stones along the track,*
> *That I should walk alone and oft-times weep,*
> *That I should stumble where I thought to leap.*
> *I must go forward — there is no way back.*

Who said the path was filled with roses fair,
That flowers bloomed and skies were never black?
They never told the thorns that roses bear,
Or that the cloudless skies would prove so rare!
I must go forward — there is no way back.

One said — 'There are no lions in the way,
It is easy going and the rein is slack'.
But never told the points where I might stray;
How long the night and yet how short the day;
— I must go forward — there is no way back.

But there was One who said, 'I'll be with thee,
Despite all wantings, thou shalt never lack.
In spite of thorns the roses thou shalt see;
And know in all thy ways My certainty;
Then just go forward and do not look back.'

What count the roses, lions, thorns or cloud;
The lightning flashing, or the thunder's crack;
The voice that calls me still is clear and loud.
He chose me, picking me from out the crowd.
— I will go forward — I would not go back."

Margaret loved people and she loved Congo. Her first term of service gave her an indescribable thrill and real satisfaction, and her dedicated personality endeared her to all. During this term she worked at the Children's Home in Stanleyville, at Maganga and, finally, at Bongondza. The only thing which marred her service was the continuing migraine attacks from which she suffered. During her first furlough she consulted the doctor, who felt she was unfit for further service abroad, and advised her to tender her resignation. It seemed as though the bottom of her world had fallen out, and with broken heart and unashamed tears she went to see the General Secretary at Headquarters. She obtained a nursing post in the homeland, though her heart still yearned for Congo, and within two years the migraine attacks ceased and she felt led to re-apply to the Mission. On passing her medical, her spirit was elated, and with renewed dedication she prepared to sail for Congo once more.

In August 1962 a letter arrived from the Field, appointing her to the village of Bopepe. She wrote, "My first reaction was one of delight, for I know most of the folk there, and it is also the village of Pastor Asani and Bo Martin — the twins. Yes, it is literally a village, lying actually alongside the main road about 50 miles from my last station and 90 miles from Stanleyville.

"The language is Bangala for which I was very glad, as those of you who know me will appreciate my language problems, and I already know Bangala!

"However, on re-reading the letter I realised with a shock that I was to start a medical work there! Do you know that feeling when it seems one's stomach has done a somersault? Well, that's how I felt on first reflection! Then quickly I remembered that it was God who had called me and He was also in the appointment, and whilst humanly speaking I feel totally inadequate for the task, with God all things are possible. Doesn't James 1 : 5 tell us, 'If any of you lack wisdom, let him ask of God, that giveth to all men liberally, and upbraideth not; and it shall be given him'?"

The next month, the General Secretary wrote his parting letter to her, reminding her that "the battle is not yours, but God's". He said, "Firstly, we must remember we are engaged in a *conflict,* a battle for righteousness, and we must note that word. Secondly, we have a *Captain,* who is God Himself and our cause is safe in His hands. Finally, there is a *choice,* whether it is ours or His. When we make it our own we see what human hands can do, but when we accept it as God's battle, we see what a Divine hand can do".

Margaret was soon installed at Bopepe and making her presence felt. The people loved her and she was never short of patients. In the last letter to her prayer partners, dated June 1964, she confessed that more than one hundred letters were awaiting an answer, but she could not even begin the task. Why was she so busy? Her letter gave the explanation, "We've had a five months' epidemic of measles, whooping cough and dysentery with all the complications they bring. The epidemic finished and things were getting more back to normal when the Bopepe birthrate went up by 50%, which made inroads on any spare time I may have had! Now don't feel sorry for me; just continue to pray harder for the Lord to thrust out more labourers into this corner of the harvest-field, or better still come out yourself!" Then she continued to give a picture of the little sick unit and dispensary in which she was privileged to work, and it was still tinged with her customary humour. "The little 12-bed ward which I have is constantly full, and the waiting room in the dispensary is now too small to hold the crowd which gathers to hear the Gospel prior to receiving treatment, and plans are in the making (though who knows when they may materialise?) for enlarging the room to hold another 50 people. The Lord is blessing the medical ministry, and many hear the Gospel because they are sick who otherwise would probably never or rarely hear. Have turned my hand again to veterinary work in that I've had to sew up two dogs, both of whom had a life and death fight with a baboon! One of the two had stolen all the eggs out of our chicken house only the week before; small wonder his owner was embarrassed to ask me to mend his dog for him!"

Margaret was at Banjwadi when the rebellion broke out but, knowing that her fellow-worker and close personal friend Mary Baker was alone at Bopepe, she made her way deeper into rebel territory to be with her. On the 3rd of November both Mary Baker and Margaret Hayes were arrested at Bopepe and taken to the town of Banalia where they joined Dr. and Mrs. Sharpe and family, Mr. and Mrs. Parry and family and Miss Ruby Gray. At Banalia the doctor and Ruby exercised a medical ministry even under the control of the rebels. During the whole of November the entire population demanded the release of Margaret in order to continue the medical work at Bopepe, as some of the villagers were urgently needing attention. They pleaded that 'Madamoiselle Marguerite' be allowed to return to the village, and eventually the Simbas gave their consent. Margaret returned on the last truck out of Banalia on the 23rd November, and on the next day the paratroopers descended on Stanleyville. On the 25th November, in vengeance the Simbas led their hostages to the river bank where they massacred all of them — shooting some and spearing others. Thus Margaret escaped on the last day by the very last vehicle. Simbas were then sent to Bopepe to arrest Margaret but the Christians, determined to protect their beloved missionary to the last, hid her in the forest where she remained in hiding for a month. The Simbas combed the woods, questioned villagers and then shot two of the church members. They threatened to annihilate the church in that village unless Margaret surrendered. Margaret heard the news and realised it was no idle threat. She felt it was better to give herself rather than allow the Body of Christ to be mutilated for her. On Christmas Eve she left her forest refuge and walked to a party of Simbas, saying, "If you want to kill me, I am ready". However, the anger of the Simbas had subsided and she was taken to Banalia where she worked as a nurse, and later to Buta where she was assigned to make epaulettes for the insurrectionists. Here she was imprisoned in the Roman Catholic convent with 31 priests, 15 nuns and a Belgian woman and her two children.

Meanwhile, friends in the homeland had given up hope that any had survived the massacre at Banalia, although none of Margaret's clothing had been found on the river bank. Thus she was in the unique position of being alive and well and living at Buta, while friends in the homeland mourned her passing, wrote her obituary, and attended the Memorial Service in Westminster Chapel, her name being listed as one of the missing, believed killed. The Mission issued Certificates of Presumed Death to the relatives in order that their Estates could be distributed. Margaret's read, "We hereby certify that Miss Margaret Hayes was known to have reported to the town of Banalia, Republic of Congo, on orders from the rebel authorities. When the relieving mercenary forces arrived at Banalia they found various items of blood-stained clothing on the river-bank, pointing to almost certain death. No trace of any of the hostages held in this town was found, and the chances of survival are virtually negligible. It is believed that the massacre took place on or about the 15th December 1964."

During March three separate letters arrived from different sources, each stating that Margaret Hayes was alive. Almost at the same time, a Simba boy, who surrendered in Stanleyville, gave news that a Mme. Beka had not been killed. At first it was thought that Mary Baker had survived, but subsequently it transpired to be Margaret Hayes. It seemed almost un-believable, but then a letter arrived from Margaret herself. The only address she gave was "Congo", but she reported that she was well and had sufficient food, and confirmed the deaths of all the others at Banalia. "Only I am left," she concluded. Two further letters were received from Margaret, one dated the 5th April and the other the 17th May, and both arrived in London on the 31st May. This time she confirmed that she was held at Buta. The first letter recorded her 40th birthday. "Today I have reached the awful age of 40 and, reading Deuteronomy 8 : 1-10 I was very amused, but how true it is that the Lord has led me these forty years. His hand has surely been upon me for good, yes, even in the trials, even in the wilderness, He was with me in it all, to prove me and to humble me. Oh that it may bring forth the fruit *He* desires!

"The sisters presented me with a magnificent bouquet at breakfast, plus a birthday card and a present. You'd never think we were prisoners-of-war! Several of the priests came over and gave their greetings too. Truly the fellowship of suffering is a very precious fellowship, for it sweeps away all barriers of language, colour and creed. Philippians 3:10 reveals the wish that we may be in fellowship with the sufferings of the Lord, but what He allows us to suffer is nothing to what He bore for us; even so, it is a privilege to have been allowed to go through these difficult days, for He has become so very much more precious; sometimes it is necessary for Him to remove *all* human props in order that we may better lean on Him Who alone is able to support us at these times.

"Apart from my Bible the only other book I possess is what I found at Banjwade, *God Holds the Key* by Geoffrey Bull (I believe the book belongs to Barrie Morris). Have found strange comfort in his (G. Bull's) writings, and the meditations are a source of great blessing to my heart. He understands how I feel now, and in moments of distress I've turned again and again to the book when it has been difficult to pray, etc."

The next letter recorded her thoughts of her parents at home who celebrated their Golden Wedding Anniversary on the 22nd April 1965, and revealed the kind fellowship with the Roman Catholic hostages at this time. But more than that her heart went out to the land of Congo and she reaffirmed her desire to continue serving in this country. "Again opportunity is given to send you word that all is well with me here, and the Lord is providing for our needs in a wonderful way. Praise Him! There has been a real break for me spiritually and truly I am experiencing more and more the consciousness of His abiding presence; I guess it is that you folk at home are praying.

"Days pass very quickly, there is usually enough to occupy one's hands during the day, and we go to bed early. I'm making the epaulettes for the "Army"; I had to wrap them in pairs, so being as I came here first as a missionary and secondarily as a prisoner, and not having a bean to my name, I asked the sisters for some small printed pictures of Christ. I chose some with Christ surrounded by people of all nations. So now each packet goes out with one of these in it: if only the recipient would turn his thoughts to Christ and pray for pardon and peace!

"The 22nd April was my parents' golden wedding (I still don't know if they are alive) however, the sisters went all out, and we celebrated royally, with poems written in English, and two songs in English (written by the priests).

"Would value your prayers for food, so far we have enough but we've only enough flour left for another week (we bake bread for 57), and meat is getting low; the priests and brothers have been without fresh meat for almost two weeks now.

"The Mother Superior has given me material to make a dress, and one of the priests also had two dresses in the attic left over from clothes sent for the 'poor of Congo'! These he graciously gave, and we've altered them, so now I am decently dressed once again!

"There are numerous opportunities for prayer and meditation, and I specially remember No. 9 and U.F.M. generally at 5.30 a.m. and again at 2.30 - 3.30. Midday, 6.30 and night I devote to the Congo field; these times are increasingly precious to me as you can guess.

"Mr. Harris, we can't leave our field high and dry! We *must* have workers, and if God wills, when and if I'm released, I would like to return. Think of the poor scattered flock of Christ! My heart breaks whenever I think of it.

"Two weeks ago I went down with a really severe attack of malaria and the sisters spoiled me; the Queen herself couldn't have had better treatment. This last week we've dysentery in the camp; I've had a light attack, but am now over it. A month ago we all weighed ourselves, and I have gained 20 lbs. out of the 30 that I lost!"

Mr. Larson and Mr. Jenkinson flew back to Congo about this time and did all they could to secure the release of Margaret. Several priests and nuns had got through the barriers and they felt that, given time, Margaret could get through as well. However, the mercenaries were building up reserves ready for another advance into the interior and it was learned that Buta was the objective, where they were hoping to secure the release of the remaining hostages. Again, much prayer went up and two platoons of mercenaries left, one from Paulis, travelling westwards, and one from Bondo, travelling eastwards. Then on Saturday, the 29th May, the worst massacre of all took place. The war was almost over, the Simba cause was dying, there seemed no reason for further bloodshed, yet as the mercenary troops drove into Buta they found more than 30 hostages had been slain, and they were only successful in rescuing a few.

Anxiously Mr. Jenkinson awaited news in Leopoldville, while the Secretaries and friends at home again called special prayer meetings, and a 'plane passage was booked in faith — but Margaret never arrived in Leopoldville.

Colonel Makondo was the Simba commandant at Buta and was just twenty-nine years of age. He could hardly write, and this service was cared for by a secretary who had been 'resurrected'. Makondo was a fierce, cruel man and not only delighted in the killing of hostages but frequently performed executions of offending Simbas. One night, in a fit of rage, he took twelve Simbas from the ranks and summarily shot them in front of their comrades, accusing them of disobeying orders. On another occasion he shot a hole in the lobe of the ear of one of his soldiers for a similar offence. His 'secretary', when a junior warrior, was sentenced to death for a misdemeanour but Colonel Makondo shot and superficially wounded him, causing the boy to faint. When his colleagues threw the 'body' into the river, the cold water revived him and Makondo ordered him to be pulled out as he had been 'resurrected', and immediately promoted him to his personal secretary. Margaret met Makondo on several occasions but he was usually polite in front of the ladies, though never let his eyes meet theirs. During her three months of captivity, she made a total of 1,500 pairs of epaulettes, mainly from a pale green cotton material obtained from the Convent and this occupied her from eight in the morning until six at night. They usually had sufficient food and were not ill treated. Margaret maintained the half-day of prayer on the first Wednesday of the month, observed throughout the Mission since foundation days. The nuns were impressed with the idea and endeavoured to leave her undisturbed for her tryst with God.

When it was known that the mercenaries were on their way to Buta, Makondo ordered the massacre of the 31 priests in his clutches and the 'arrest' of the ladies. About eleven in the morning a mob of Simbas arrived armed with spears, shouting and yelling, and their intentions were obvious. Could it be that the mercenaries were already within shooting distance? They locked the doors and turned out the lights, hoping to 'hold on' for a short while. But the Mother Superior ordered the doors to be opened and the ladies were marched over to the Fathers' quarters and then on to the Post Office building. The priests were taken from their quarters and brutally beaten. They took the beating very bravely with scarcely a cry or shout and the punishment lasted until four in the afternoon. They were then given the special Simba torture. Their arms were crossed behind their backs and tied at the elbows. Similarly, the legs were crossed and tied at the ankles and knees. Then a rope was passed around the elbows and ankles and the ankles were drawn up, forcing the body into a backward arch, into an extremely painful position. For the first time the priests cried in agony. Water was poured on the knots to make them fast, and later the ropes were cut and they were marched to the river bank. A Simba stood at the door of the room where the ladies were held and gave a running commentary on the proceedings. The priests were then attacked with machettes, killed, and thrown into the river. The Simba guard passed one of the mutilated legs around and forced everyone to handle it. One of the children asked what sort of an animal it was. Her mother replied she did not know, it was just "something from the forest".

During this period of 'close arrest' the Simba guards became more brutal to their captives, no doubt in vengeance for the series of defeats which they had suffered. Their rations were reduced and they had only river water to drink. They were not allowed to pray, and one nun caught with her hands clasped was roughly knocked with the shaft of a spear and told, "There is only one god and that is Lumumba".

On the 31st May the mercenaries were in Buta, only five miles away from the place where the ladies were concealed. How they longed to get a message through, but this seemed impossible. The mercenaries had advanced along two roads, and then searched the third running south to Banalia, hoping to catch up with the Simbas and their hostages who they thought were fleeing. A short distance out of Buta is a little insignificant track known as the Basali trail, and it was down this track that the ladies were taken. After crossing a stream, the Simbas destroyed the tree trunk bridge and when the mercenaries searched the Basali trail they went as far as the stream and did not consider it worthwhile going further. Less than half a mile away 19 women waited anxiously. They heard their would-be rescuers calling for them over loud speakers, but they sat in deathly silence looking at the pointed guns of their captors. One false move at this juncture would have meant the death of them all!

There seemed to be little hope for Margaret. It seemed impossible that she had survived the second massacre. Then, a month later, a Congolese discovered their whereabouts and informed the mercenaries. He led them through the forest and suggested they did not fire as they went, as they usually did. Margaret was sitting looking out of the hut, waiting, watching and wondering, when suddenly, almost too suddenly to realise what was happening, a platoon of white soldiers burst over the summit of the hillock in her view and charged, with rifles raining bullets, down the slope. The Simbas fled. The ladies burst into tears, and were free.

Margaret suffered two horrifying experiences, was under the constant threat of death for ten months, saw blood shed, sadism and hatred unleashed, yet, as she flew home for a rest and to see her relatives, she re-dedicated her life to God and His work in Congo.

Margaret Hayes has the faith of a saint, the compassion of Christ, and the mind of a missionary, "As soon as the situation has stabilised in the Congo, I want to return to those I call my own people, for in spite of all that has happened I feel that my place is among those I can serve best. When once you have dedicated yourself to God's work there's NO WAY BACK." How different from the traditional mentality of the Congolese who kill their enemies in vengeance and eat them in anger. Remember the crocodile. But with missionaries like Margaret, Christ's own teaching of "Love your enemies, bless them that curse you, do good to them which hate you, and pray for them which despitefully use you, and persecute you", is gradually being taught, and the Church of Jesus Christ established.

Christ's better way of life has triumphed again and goes on triumphing. Soon the blood and suffering attached to the saga of Margaret Hayes will be but a record on the pages of history but her love and compassion will live on — as long as the work of the Mission continues — for from His love there is no way back.

THE UNEVANGELIZED FIELDS MISSION is a faith mission, working in Brazil, British Guiana, Dominican Republic, France, Haiti, Ivory Coast, Java, Papua and West Irian, as well as the Congo Republic.

Information regarding the fields can be obtained from the General Secretary, Unevangelized Fields Mission, 9 Gunnersbury Avenue, London, W.5.

If you have been blessed while reading *Congo Saga,* you may like to obtain other U.F.M. publications:

BRAZIL

Long Climb on the Xingu	Horace Banner	3s. 6d.
Amazon Moon	Rosemary Cunningham	2s. 6d.
Vera Cruz (for children)	Leonard Harris	2s. 6d.
The Three Freds (for children — painting and cut-out book)	Horace Banner	2s. 6d.
Mischievous Maria (for children — painting book)	David Truby	1s. 0d.
Battle for the Big-Lips	S. V. Poultney	4s. 6d.

CONGO

Congo Snapshots	S. V. Poultney	4s. 6d.
The Twins (for children)	S. V. Poultney	1s. 6d.
Twimp (for children — painting book)	David Truby	1s. 0d.

IVORY COAST

So this is Ivory Coast!	David Truby	1s. 6d.
God's Little Helper (For children painting book)	David Truby	1s. 0d.

PAPUA AND WEST IRIAN

Out of the Dark	Shirley Horne	5s. 0d·
The Battle for the Bigwigs	Eva Twyman	5s. 0d.
Past Finding Out	Joan E. Rule	9d.

GENERAL

Our Days in His Hands (History of the Mission)	Leonard Harris	4s. 6d.

POSTAGE EXTRA

MAGAZINE

Light and Life (published quarterly— contains news from all the Fields)	per annum 5s. 0d.